D1193003

Understanding Asexuality

Understanding Asexuality

Anthony F. Bogaert

ROWMAN & LITTLEFIELD PUBLISHERS, INC.
Lanham • Boulder • New York • Toronto • Plymouth, UK

Published by Rowman & Littlefield Publishers, Inc.
A wholly owned subsidiary of The Rowman & Littlefield Publishing Group, Inc.
4501 Forbes Boulevard, Suite 200, Lanham, Maryland 20706
www.rowman.com

10 Thornbury Road, Plymouth PL6 7PP, United Kingdom

British Library Cataloguing in Publication Information Available

Library of Congress Cataloging-in-Publication Data

Bogaert, Anthony F., 1963–
Understanding asexuality / Anthony F. Bogaert.
p. cm.
ISBN 978-1-4422-0099-9 (cloth : alk. paper) — ISBN 978-1-4422-0101-9 (electronic)
1. Sex. 2. Gender identity. I. Title.
HQ21.B754 2012
305.8—dc23
2012009164

Printed in the United States of America

Contents

Acknowledgments

A sincere thanks to the following people who helped at various stages of the development of this book: Carolyn Hafer, Sasha Noorgaard, Malvina Skorska, and the editorial staff at Rowman & Littlefield. Your support and generosity are greatly appreciated. I would also like acknowledge the love and support of my mother and father throughout the years; my academic career would not have been possible without them.

For LB.

ONE

Introduction

I teach and research human sexuality in two academic departments—the Department of Community Health Sciences and the Department of Psychology—at Brock University in the Niagara region of Canada. My university is supportive, and I expect that most of my university colleagues respect my work, but a few of my fellow professors are a bit dismissive of what I do. Some joke about what *must* go on in my human sexuality courses (e.g., "Your small-group seminars must be quite the party!" or "I bet there's a lot of *hands-on* learning in your courses!"). Others tout my courses as the first to deserve a "little trimming" when university budgets are subject to cutbacks, the suggestion being that sex is taking up too much of the undergraduate curriculum, when, of course, more important and pithy matters could (and should!) supplant it. Still others question the utility of government grants being earmarked for the study of human sexuality.

Why do some of my colleagues treat my research and courses this way? I imagine that they do so, partly, out of a lingering notion that sexual activities, including teaching and research about sexual activities, have to do with the unseemly, the naughty, or at least the "unserious" side of life. I expect that the seed of this notion is sown very early in the lives of most Westerners (including in these few nonsupportive colleagues), germinates and reaches its peak during adolescence, and then persists in some form into adulthood. In fact, evidence of the persistence of this notion is charming, to a degree, when I witness my (usually male) colleagues revisit the raunchy side of their adolescence and engage in sex banter over a few beers.

I also imagine that these colleagues feel this way because they, like many of their fellow baby boomers, have slipped unawares into their current stage of life: middle age. (By the way, I have also reached this milestone, and have started to label it, somewhat bitterly, as the stage of "middle-aged ugly." I call it so because, alas, our beauty—what little we may have had of it—has now faded, and we are saggy and increasingly hairless geeks.[1] Cruel as it may be, fickle Hollywood, with its eyes fixed on beauty, has begun to give us the cold shoulder.) For some of my colleagues, with the best of their youthful charms and vigor behind them, sex is now increasingly off the radar, and a somewhat "de-sexualized" worldview holds sway. This reflects, of course, a natural transition most adults experience as middle-aged bodies start to change and preoccupations shift to other fancies, including, say, helping one's children negotiate their lives. The famous psychoanalyst, Erik Erikson, aptly summarized this life stage as one preoccupied with generativity: the care of future generations (Stevens, 1983).

But some of my middle-aged colleagues' newfound worldview has—yikes!—begun to undermine my work, as they have now started to give me looks and behave as if they have had an epiphany on academic values: *Why should the study of sex matter so much, when for the vast majority of the moments in our lives, we are not engaged in it, and when the majority of our thoughts and preoccupations are not confined to this rather strange activity, even though, granted, they may have been years ago?*

Well, maybe these colleagues are right. Why does sex matter so much? It is true that the vast majority of our lives, even during periods when our lives are extremely sexualized, is not spent engaging in sex. For example, in any given day, much more time is spent eating, watching TV, grooming, or sleeping than having sex. Indeed, sex does not even rate as an identifiable category when activities of the day are tallied (Longley, n.d.). Note that I am assuming a straightforward interpretation of these activities and not one more favorable to a turf-defending sexologist, who might argue that such tallies often do not take into account "hidden" time devoted to sex, such as viewing sexualized content on TV or other media, or "inner-life" activities such as sexual fantasizing. But no, let's not quibble. It is true that sexual activities do not take much of the day at all, even if we include "hidden" sex time. So, what is all the fuss about?

In the 1970s, psychologists became more academically interested in human sexuality. This occurred for a number of reasons, not the least of which was that the sexual world opened up personally and scientifically in the wake of the 1960s sexual revolution. At that time, two publications by two social psychologists, Zick Rubin and Donn Byrne, put forward some convincing arguments that all the fuss about sex was in fact worth it, scientifically speaking (Rubin, 1973; Byrne, 1977). They catalogued a number of reasons for the importance of studying (and teaching about) sexuality. Here are some of their choice examples,[2] along with a few of my own.

Sex is intrinsically interesting to most people, even to those who are not in the reproductive prime of their lives. That my middle-aged colleagues often still turn to the subject of sex after a few beers is evidence that they are still interested in sex, even if their daily lives may contain little behavior that is actually sexual. The prevalence of sexual allusions, if not outright sexual content, in the media also attests to the fact that sex is capable of arousing curiosity in, along with titillating, the young and old alike. In 2010, the most "Googled" person was not the president of the United States or the pope, but Lady Gaga, the pop music star with a hyper-sexed persona.

The level of scientific curiosity about sex is also high, despite some of my colleagues' views. There is a 553-page book (at least in the first edition) called *The Female Orgasm* (Fisher, 1973), and not even a small pamphlet on the female sneeze. Yet both an orgasm and a sneeze entail similar physiological processes: a buildup of muscular tension released in contorting spasm(s). There must be more intrinsic interest in the former than the latter, even among us (usually) disinterested scientists, to explain the disparity in research. Finally, my courses do not suffer from a paucity of student interest—a fact that even my most skeptical colleagues cannot ignore; indeed, sex courses are often the most popular offerings on college campuses.

In short, sex is very interesting to most of us, so why not study and learn about a subject that piques human curiosity? I think this "high level of interest/curiosity" argument is a convincing one, assuming that all else is equal in terms of sex's scientific importance and health implications relative to other domains of life. But some of you are surely thinking, *Aye, there's the rub, because all else is not equal. Sex may pique our curiosity, but it is not on par with other domains of life in its scientific importance or its health implications!*

I beg to differ. In terms of scientific importance, sex is on par with, or even trumps, some of the biggest scientific puzzles. Not only do we not fully understand why sex exists (i.e., why some species, for example, reproduce using male and female forms; see chapter 3), but sex is often the clue to unravelling the mystery of a species as a whole, or at least it is never ignored when biologists (e.g., zoologists) study a species as a whole. The same can be said for the study of humans. To understand our sexuality is to understand ourselves. There is an ancient Chinese proverb that says, "To understand the head, one must begin by studying the tail." (Using an animal metaphor to make its point, this proverb is, of course, meant to reveal the secret to understanding human beings.) Sigmund Freud, the famous psychoanalyst, and evolutionary psychologists (strange bedfellows, indeed!) have thought similarly, suggesting that sex is the major scientific puzzle of human nature, and that to understand sex is to understand human beings. So, the *hows* and *whys* of the way we think, feel, and behave are determined, arguably, by our sexuality.

However, one does not have to resort to arguing from the scientific value of decoding the mystery of human nature to make the point that sex is an important academic pursuit. Sex clearly has a profound effect on humans on practical levels. Consider two sisters who are close in age but who differ in their sexual orientation, one being straight and the other lesbian. Will their life trajectories be the same? The answer is, of course, in some ways, yes, but in many others, no. The sisters ultimately will have very different lives, in large part because of their differing sexual orientations. Sexual orientation—like many components of sexuality— plays a profound role in our social circumstances and life choices, including whether we marry, where we live, or whether we have children. For example, the majority of heterosexual women give birth to children and the majority of lesbians do not. Data from the National Survey of Family Growth (NSFG) in 2002 confirm this, with 65 percent of heterosexual and bisexual women having given birth to a child, compared to 35 percent of lesbians. Thus, the study of sexuality is clearly relevant to a variety of scientific disciplines, including demography (Baumle, in press), which attempts to understand trends related to marriage and fertility, among other issues.

Beyond basic scientific interests, sexuality also relates to health and social issues, often profoundly so. The list of relevant health and social ills is long: overpopulation, environmental degradation, gender inequality, sexually transmitted infections/diseases, divorce/family disruption, and marital and child abuse. Take, for example, the issues of overpopulation and the environment. Does anyone think that these are not affected by people's sexuality (e.g., their contraception practices)? This is not to say that sex is the only contributing factor to these and other health and social issues, but rather that all of them are affected by human sexuality, and for some of these issues, the case could be made that sexuality is the underlying factor in their development. Thus, if one truly wants to improve the world, sex is a subject that cannot to be ignored.

So, the fuss about sex is well deserved. Sex affects much of our lives, and its meaning and ramifications do not just have to do with the "act" itself. At a most basic level, sex is about human life. Interestingly, major health organizations such as the World Health Organization (WHO) are recognizing the central role of sexuality in human life, along with the myriad of ways it impacts health. Consider WHO's (n.d.) working definition: "Sexuality is a central aspect of being human and encompasses sex, gender identities and roles, orientation, eroticism, pleasure, intimacy and reproduction."

At this point you may be wondering whether I am perhaps inadvertently undermining the task ahead: to convince the reader that asexuality is an important scientific inquiry. Note that when I refer here to asexuality, I mean the real deal—that is, a complete lack of sexual attraction and/or sexual interest (see chapter 2 on definitions)—and not just a middle-age, on-again, off-again malaise about sex, as mentioned above. And so, given sexuality's central importance in human life, is it then true that *hard-core* asexuality (if I am permitted this description), if it is the opposite of sexuality, must be unimportant, a nonissue, a mere footnote in the great (sexual) story of life? Why *does* the study of asexuality matter?

There are many reasons why it matters. In fact, I think the study of asexuality matters so much that I was compelled to write this book on it. Here are some of my reasons why asexuality matters and why I am writing this book.

First, there is value in the opportunity for members of an overlooked and under-studied population to be able to read about and understand issues relevant to them. Thus asexual people might be interested in finding out more about themselves, and this is reason enough to write a book on asexuality. This is not a new concept: books are written about (and to) specialized audiences all the time.

But this book is written not just for asexual people, or even just for research scientists studying asexual people. It is also written for anyone interested in learning more about sexuality. For example, a book on asexuality may satisfy curiosity—both scientific and public—about a sexual minority that has been overlooked until recently. Thus many readers will get a chance to peek into and learn more about a world that is sexually different from theirs. Aside from satisfying curiosity, such glimpses into new worlds may have health and social benefits, as exposure to sexual minorities may help to increase general tolerance and acceptance. This idea—called the "contact hypothesis" of prejudice reduction—is often associated with psychologist Gordon Allport (1954), but the original theory has been extended beyond personal contact to encompass exposure through the media, including books (Cameron & Rutland, 2006).

A book about asexuality is also a book about sex (how could it be otherwise?), and therefore many of the reasons listed above to study sex apply equally well to the study of asexuality. For example, recall that one of the reasons to study sex is that it informs a number of scientific disciplines, including demography, which studies, among other things, fertility and marriage. There are no published data on the fertility of asexual people (a topic well worth looking into), but in the first published study on asexuality using a national probability (or random) sample of adults in Great Britain, I found that 33 percent of asexual people were currently in a long-term relationship (e.g., married), compared to 64 percent of sexual people (Bogaert, 2004). Thus, the study of asexuality reveals how variations in sexuality profoundly affect one's (demographically relevant) life trajectories.

There is another equally important reason to study asexuality that has not yet been mentioned. Asexuality offers us a unique opportunity to look at sexuality through a new lens, affording perhaps a clearer (or at least new) view of what sex is and what it is not. In fact, this is one of the reasons why asexuality is interesting to a sexologist like me: It reveals hidden truths about sex. In the same way that homosexuality allows us to understand heterosexuality, and vice versa, asexuality allows us to make broad comparisons to understand sexuality as a whole. This is also why a book on asexuality matters.

In support of my argument, consider further the example above: 33 percent of asexual people were found to be in long-term relationships, compared to 64 percent of sexual people. Again, this information provides evidence that life circumstances often differ between asexual and sexual people, but in these figures (in particular, the 33 percent for asexual people), there is also something interesting revealed or at least suggested about the nature of human sexuality and romance.

We often use the words "sex" (or "sexuality") and "romance" synonymously; in other words, sex equals romance and romance equals sex. "Romance" is perhaps the softer, gentler, and euphemistic word for "sex" (more on the meanings of romance in chapter 2), but the two words are often used interchangeably. In commercials for an erectogenic drug, advertisers tell men to "Buy Discount Cialis and Enjoy a Romantic Weekend" (ED Pills, 2010 March 30). Of course, we all know what that means: Use this drug and there is plenty of sex ahead, boys! Indeed, the ad goes on to suggest that "With a single pop of Cialis, you will not only enjoy a romantic night; expect a weekend of sizzling nights with your beloved." So, romance equals sex.

But are romantic relationships always the same thing as sexual relationships (or, to put it somewhat more complexly, does romance always imply a sexual component)? Recently, some psychologically and evolutionarily minded theorists have argued that sex and romance, although often co-occurring, are two different things. These theorists argue that the brain architecture and cognitive processing for lustful attractions emerged at a very different time in evolutionary history than those for romantic attachments (Fisher, 2004). Romance may have evolved relatively recently in our evolutionary history, developing out of processes related to how children attach themselves to parents (Hazan & Shaver, 1987). So, over evolutionary time, the brain architecture and processing originally reserved for securely attaching ourselves to our mothers—a good thing—has been co-opted and modified to allow us also to attach ourselves to our romantic partners. Presto: romantic love is born! In contrast, our faculty for sexual desire and attraction ("the lust system") may have evolved from the ancient animal mating and sexual attraction systems, much older neuropsychological systems than the attachment system in the brain. So what are we to make of asexual people who form long-term (and presumably) "romantic" relationships (33 percent)? The fact that many asexual people, who presumably do not operate from a lust/sexual attraction perspective, have an operating romantic-attraction system gives support to the idea that the sexual attraction and romantic attraction systems are indeed different. Thus, asexuals who are in relationships and have romantic attachments to their partners are an important *test case* of the theory that sexual and romantic attraction can potentially operate independently. Asexuals are not necessarily *a*romantic. Hence, the nature of sex (and romance) can be revealed by studying asexuality.

The study of asexuality offers a unique opportunity to view sexuality through a new lens, but, perhaps more importantly, this new lens affords a distant, wide-angle view of its subject. When scientists examine a phenomenon, they often try to remove themselves from it so that they can view it more objectively—to view their earthly phenomenon as if they were, perhaps, looking down from space. Asexuality may provide this kind of distance from sexuality. So getting an asexual person's view on sex, and/or trying to see sex from an asexual perspective, allows us to see sex in a new way.

In chapter 8, I show that adopting this distant view of sex offers us some intriguing insights into the nature of human sexuality. One of these insights is that sex is odd, if not downright bizarre. For example, when we deconstruct the sex act—certainly easier to do if one is asexual—its components can be perceived as "symptoms" suitable to a diagnosis of a mental disorder: obsessive thoughts, odd vocalizations, repetitive movements, and so forth. This illustration may strike you as a bit strained (albeit perhaps amusing), but I expect that with some thought, the main point of this deconstruction of sex is understood. Also, even if not convinced by this illustration, other evidence exists, as shown in chapter 8, that sexuality is often linked to strange and even pathological behaviors. So, despite sex being the "great story of life," it is also sometimes tenuously linked to mental health, broadly defined. These connections certainly make me wonder about what is a disorder, sexual and otherwise, and whether, for example, asexuality should be construed as one (Bogaert, 2006b; Bogaert, 2008) (see also chapter 9). In any event, I think the odd world of sex is worth exploring, especially as viewed from the distance of an asexual person.

A distant view of sex offered up by asexuality also shows how pervasive sexuality is in our own and many other cultures and how very profoundly it affects people's lives. (Ironically, perhaps some critics of human sexuality research need to take a true asexual's view of sexuality to see how important sex is in its effects on people and society!) For example, in chapter 11, I show how sexuality pervades the media, including art, and speculate on what the history of art, and aesthetics generally, would be like without sex. Similarly, in chapter 12, I discuss humor, this strange and wonderful faculty of the human psyche; I review why so much humor is sexually oriented and what humor would be like if it was completely devoid of sex. I also ponder the degree to which asexual people "get" sexual humor. Again, the asexual view on these issues leads to important insights into sex and human nature generally, and thus adopting an "asexual" lens affords a view we shouldn't miss. So stick around: I expect the ride will be an interesting one.

NOTES

1. I know that I am being an ageist to suggest that youth is synonymous with physical beauty. Well, to all you middle-aged people like me who think I am being ageist, all I have to say is this: *Act your age!* Attractiveness can be construed as the amount of draw or attention we can pull from others, and I think there are two age-sensitive, attention-getting components of attractiveness/beauty. First, there is a child-like "cuteness" component, which draws attention from others and is important because of its role in attaining the attention/care that children receive from competent others, such as parents. Thus, children have beauty in the form of "cuteness" that adults find appealing, because children need to draw adult attention to themselves in order to be cared for. As such, adults who retain some of this cuteness (e.g., boyish charm) can still draw their share of attention from others. The second youth-based component of beauty is related to fertility and reproductive vigor. Adolescents and adults need to draw the attention of others to reproduce, so it is not surprising that body and face features we find appealing are often cues to these characteristics. Furthermore, most people's fertility and reproductive vigor (particularly that of women) peak in their twenties. So, alas, beauty is heavily youth based! We will discuss beauty and attractiveness in this book, as they also relate, obviously, to both sexuality and asexuality.

2. I thank the eminent sexologist, William Fisher, who introduced me to the articles by Rubin and Byrne, and who I believe mentioned some of these examples in one or more of his human sexuality lectures, which I attended as a graduate student.

TWO

The A, B, C, and Ds of Sex (and Asex)

In this second chapter, I examine some of the fundamental psychological processes of sexuality as they relate to both sexual and asexual people. These processes are rather conveniently summarized by the letters A, B, C, and D. There are two words for A: *attraction* and *arousal*. There is one B: *behavior*. C refers to *cognition*, a fancy word for our thoughts. And the fourth is D: *desire*. Focusing on these processes will allow us to deconstruct or break down and examine some of the key components of sexuality; this approach will also allow us to consider definitions of asexuality.

Let's begin with *attraction*. It refers to that rather basic, even primal, lure that draws us to someone or something. Of course, in a general (nonsexual) sense, we can be "attracted" to nearly anything—for some reason, French fries come to mind—but, for our purposes, let us keep our discussion of attraction relevant to the domains of love and sex. But here, too, we need to make a distinction between *romantic* and *sexual* attraction. Psychologist Lisa Diamond (2003b) describes romantic love as the "feelings of infatuation and emotional attachment" associated with pair bonding. This type of attraction, then, refers to the "love" attraction we have for others, and the people we find "attractive" (our objects of desire) are those with whom we may fall in love. This kind of attraction is often the stuff of drama, as many of the most powerful and enduring stories give us a heavy dose of love attraction between partners.

In contrast, sexual attraction refers to the "sexual" or lust lure for others. It also might be termed one's "sexual orientation." Sex researchers, particularly those with a psychological bent, believe that sexual attraction to others is the *sine qua non* of sexual orientation. So, for example, if you are a woman and primarily lust after—in other words, are turned on by being with, looking at, thinking about, or fantasizing about—men, then you have a *heterosexual* sexual orientation. Thus, you are *sexually attracted* to, or have sexual orientation toward, men.

The distinction between romantic and sexual attraction extends even further. As introduced in chapter 1, some biologists and social scientists have suggested that romantic and sexual processes are potentially independent, governed by different brain systems, and evolved from different processes (Diamond, 2003b; Fisher, 2004). Key aspects of romantic functioning (e.g., affectional bonding) may have evolved relatively recently in our evolutionary history from the attachment system (Hazan & Shaver, 1987), whereas sexual desire/attraction processes may have evolved from very basic mating and sexual attraction systems. The basic mating system is much older, evolutionarily (or phylogenetically) speaking, than the attachment system. Reptilian brains are, after all, geared for sex, not for love.[1]

There is a relatively famous *Seinfeld* episode—and aren't almost all of the episodes famous now?—in which the main character, Jerry, develops a romantic, but not a sexual, crush on a major league baseball player he meets (Keith Hernandez). The humor of the episode emerges from the fact that Jerry begins to behave toward Keith as he might toward a female romantic partner (e.g., infatuation, jealousy, feeling spurned). The episode illustrates how humans have the capacity to decouple romantic from sexual attraction. It also illustrates that one's romantic inclination (e.g., to a man) may, in fact, be in contrast to one's typical sexual orientation (e.g., to women).

This distinction between romantic and sexual attraction may seem clear, but the two kinds of attraction are, as most people realize, also intricately related, and they often overlap. After all—Jerry's romantic fling with Keith Hernandez notwithstanding—one's romantic attractions (e.g., to men) are usually the same as one's sexual attractions (e.g., to men). So, if I lust after Bob, I very well may also have romantic feelings for him; indeed, I may even love him. This is partly because these two attraction processes influence one another, so a sexual infatuation may ultimately turn into a romantic bond lasting a lifetime, and a romantic bond may lead to sexual attraction. Lisa Diamond (2003b) suggests that this latter sequence—love followed by lust—is more likely to occur in women than in men.

You may be thinking, *The complex relationship between romantic and sexual attraction is interesting, but what does it have to do with asexuality?* Well, nearly everything, actually. One of the main definitions of asexuality is a *lack of sexual attraction*. In the first study examining asexuality in a large national sample, which I conducted in 2004, asexuality was defined as never having felt sexual attraction to men, women, or both (Bogaert, 2004; Bogaert, 2006b). AVEN (Asexuality Visibility and Education Network), the largest website devoted to asexual issues, also defines asexuality as a lack of sexual attraction. So, many asexual people have no sexual attraction to others, meaning that there is no "lust lure" for others.[2]

Does this mean that asexual people are not romantically attracted to others? The answer to this question—"not necessarily"—should be clear, given our discussion of the distinction between romantic and sexual attraction, and the fact that they can be decoupled. As mentioned in chapter 1, a lack of sexual attraction is not the same as a lack of romantic attraction, and *asexual* is not synonymous with *aromantic*. Some asexual people demonstrate that you can have one without the other. So, if one defines asexuality as a lack of sexual attraction to others, one should also be aware that it is not necessarily defined as a lack of romantic attraction to others. As also mentioned in the opening chapter, asexuality allows us to understand sexuality, and the distinction between romantic and sexual attraction is a good example of this. Sex and romance are often linked, but not inextricably so.

I often get media requests a few weeks before Valentine's Day to discuss sexuality research. A discussion of human sexuality makes for an interesting news story, generally speaking, but it is pure gold on February 14. In early February 2010, I had a slew of reporters asking about the distinction between romantic and sexual attraction, and how it relates to asexuality. Can there be love without sex? And vice versa? For some reason, that year the media requests were all from Spanish-speaking countries—Spain, naturally, and a number from South America. I did one telephone interview for a national radio show in Colombia, using a translator. I was asked whether the decoupling of sex from love was a modern phenomenon. I suggested that, although it is not a new phenomenon, its manifestation (or how this decoupling plays itself out in human behavior) may take different forms, depending on the time period and the culture. As an example, I explained the relatively modern Western trend of people hooking up and maintaining "sex-only" relationships. To describe this trend, I used the rather indelicate but often-heard phrase *fuck buddies*. The interview ended very quickly after that, my assumption that this broadcast was not a live one (and thus could be edited, if deemed necessary) being, evidently, incorrect.

The distinction between romantic and sexual attraction is important, but its full implication is not recognized. For example, some definitions of sexual orientations not only include a sexual attraction component but also a romantic (or equivalent) one. Take the well-used textbook on sexuality, *Understanding Human Sexuality* (Hyde, DeLamater, & Byers, 2009). This text defines sexual orientation as a "person's erotic and emotional orientation towards members of his or her own gender or members of the other gender" (p. 431). This definition goes beyond "erotic" or what would be termed "sexual" attraction and includes an emotional component, suggesting that romantic attachments are important to how we define a sexual orientation. In some sense, this type of definition is a broad description for one's "gender" orientation for love, sex, or both. And it is true, as mentioned above, that romantic and erotic attachments are often closely linked. But including an emotional/romantic element in the definition is also problematic, because (as mentioned above) these types of attraction are separate phenomena, and some people don't have sexual inclinations that match their romantic inclinations.

In fact, I think that people often use their romantic inclinations to guide their self-identifications about their sexual orientation. So even if they do not have sexual attractions to one sex or another, their romantic inclinations toward one sex or another determine whether they self-identify as homosexual, heterosexual, or bisexual. I think this is often the case for asexual people, particularly if they are not "out." Young and/or closeted asexual people may still self-identify as, say, heterosexual when asked on an anonymous questionnaire about their sexual orientation, even though in a vague sense they may not feel that this label fully captures who they are as people. Again, in some sense, such people may understand "sexual orientation" more broadly to include their love/gender orientation. If so, the true number of asexuals (i.e., those lacking in sexual attraction) may be underestimated (Bogaert, in press-a; Chasin, 2011). From my perspective, these "romantic" asexual people don't have a (traditional) sexual orientation, although they do have a romantic orientation. Interestingly, many contributors to AVEN, who are privy to and often discuss the latest scientific work on sexuality, have recently picked up on the romantic/sexual distinction, and have begun to self-identify in the complex way that this distinction engenders. So, for example, it is not unusual for an asexual person to say that he is asexual but *bi*romantic, or that she is asexual but *hetero*romantic.

Let's move on to the other A: *arousal*. This usually refers to the physical aspects of one's sexual response, or what happens in the genitals when sexual stimuli are encountered (e.g., stroking of the inner thigh, or imagining a sexy scene). So this aspect is less psychological, at least in comparison to attraction, and more physical, referring primarily to bodily responses such as erections and vaginal changes (lubrication). Because these physical changes are detectable, there has been a tradition in sexology of researchers measuring psychophysical sexual arousal. The man who pioneered the technique in the 1950s was Kurt Freund (sounds like Freud but isn't), a Czech/Canadian who was primarily interested in seeing if men were gay or straight. Later he used this technique to measure deviant arousal in male sexual offenders. The original device used to measure physical arousal was a specialized elastic tube placed around the flaccid penis, which measured changes in blood flow as a man gained an erection. Still later, in the 1960s, a psychophysical device—a tampon-like cylinder inserted in the vagina, also measuring genital blood flow—was developed for women. Today, these techniques, or modern variations of them, are relatively widely used (at least among sexologists!) to assess sexual arousal in men and women in a variety of circumstances.

There is also a subjective or purely psychological component to arousal. Most people have a sense of their own arousal ("feeling" aroused), and this can be simply measured by asking someone, for example, "How aroused or turned on are you by what you are watching?" People will typically use their own genital changes as a marker, but there is not necessarily a perfect correspondence between physical changes and psychological arousal. This is particularly true for women, for whom subjective arousal often does not match bodily changes that may or may not be occurring (Heiman, 1977). Thus, there can be an arousal disconnect between what happens in our bodies and what happens in our minds.

How are arousal and attraction related? Typically, our level of arousal, both physical and subjective, reflects our sexual attractions. So, if Joe is sexually attracted to women, then his physical arousal patterns (i.e., erections) will likely correspond to that fact. That is, he is going to be aroused in the presence of women, especially if they are attractive, unclothed, and/or engaging in sex with him. Indeed, because of this reasonable linkage between our arousal and attractions, psychophysical measures have often been used for detecting a person's deep-seated attractions, including whether the person is gay or straight. But, given that there is a potential decoupling between physical and subjective arousal (particularly in women), there is also a potential disconnect between one's physical arousal and one's attractions. So, this physical arousal cannot necessarily be seen as a mirror reflecting one's basic attractions, especially in women. Even in men, there can a decoupling between attraction and arousal. Men can have spontaneous erections without having a corresponding attraction to an object of desire. For example, a man may wake up with a morning erection without necessarily having an object of desire prompting its appearance. So, one can have a mere physical arousal experience not necessarily attached to an attraction object, or for that matter to even subjective arousal.

Again, you may be thinking, *What does all this have to do with asexuality?* Well, plenty. First, if a common definition of asexuality is experiencing a lack of sexual attraction, being asexual doesn't necessarily mean that one is incapable of being sexually aroused. In fact, for many asexual people, physical arousal is not an issue. As one asexual person describes, "I did, you know, test the equipment . . . and everything works fine, pleasurable and all, it's just not actually attracted to anything" (Brotto, Knudson, Inskip, Rhodes, & Erskine, 2010, p. 612). Note that this quote also suggests that there may be subjective arousal as well: knowing that one's body is aroused and even liking this feeling (pleasure). In short, a lack of sexual attraction does not automatically mean a lack of physical or subjective arousal.

Having finished with the two A words of sex, let's move on to B: *behavior*. Behavior is what we do—that is, our actions. There are a variety of overtly sexual activities, both solitary and partnered: masturbation, fondling, oral sex, intercourse, and so forth. However, it is not just the acts themselves but also with whom we do them that comprises our sexual behavior. Thus, a sex researcher interested in behavior may ask participants about their frequency of oral sex and also with whom they do this activity (e.g., men, women, or both). Indeed, there has been a tradition in the social sciences to use behavior as the main focus of study or interest, or as the key *dependent variable*. People's thoughts and feelings were not of primary interest, in large part because it was felt that these aspects of the mind, although obviously important, were not amenable to clear measurement. Alfred Kinsey, the twentieth century's well-known pioneer of human sexuality, was of this tradition and was most comfortable with assessing and discussing (sexual) behavior. It is not surprising that his famous books have the word *behavior* in the titles: *Sexual Behavior in the Human Male* and *Sexual Behavior in the Human Female* (Kinsey, Pomeroy, & Martin, 1948; Kinsey, Pomeroy, Martin, & Gebhard, 1953).

Kinsey described people's sexual orientation on a point scale from zero to six, again mostly based on their behavior (what they did and with whom). Kinsey *sixes* are exclusively gay/lesbian, while Kinsey *zeroes* are designated as exclusively heterosexual. Those in the middle (e.g., two to four) were designated as bisexual. This scale assumes that all people have a high level of sexual interest in their preferred sexual partners. Thus, it does not accommodate asexuality. However, Kinsey did have a name for those who just didn't fit on this scale: *X*s. So, at a party (okay, a rather unusual party), someone asks, "Are you a Kinsey *zero* (exclusively straight)? Perhaps a Kinsey *three* (bisexual)? Or perhaps a Kinsey *six* (exclusively gay)?" An asexual person schooled in the Kinsey scheme may reply, "Well, actually, I am a Kinsey *X*."

Most modern sexologists—and, for that matter, social scientists (e.g., psychologists, sociologists)—believe that the study of behavior by itself is too limiting. They happily include in their research the mind's other key processes, including its attractions, thoughts, and desires. These other aspects of the mind are widely accepted today, in part because we now have better ways of measuring them. Modern sex researchers also know that making conclusions about people based only on behavior is often fraught with problems. Here's an example. Let's say you know a man who has had in his lifetime one sexual partner, his wife, with whom he has sexual intercourse once a week. Based on this behavior, you should conclude that his sexual orientation is heterosexual. And yet, somehow, you later find out that this man's sexual fantasies (reflecting his attractions), including while having sex with his wife, are exclusively of men. A shocker, to be sure! Later, you notice that, when drunk at parties, he also seems to stare rather longingly at attractive men.[3] So, what is his sexual orientation: still heterosexual? I know no one who would suggest that this man is, in fact, heterosexual. This is because people implicitly

believe that one's deep-seated sexual attractions always trump overt behavior when attempting to understand the essence of a human being's
sexual orientation. Most modern sexual orientation researchers agree
(Bailey, Dunne, & Martin, 2000; Bogaert, 2003; Storms, 1980; Money, 1988;
Zucker & Bradley, 1995). They suggest that if we want to know whether
someone is gay or straight, we should assess his or her attractions (and
not necessarily his or her behaviors). In actuality, having more information, rather than less (including information about behavior), is important, but if you were to rely on only one aspect in assessing someone's
sexual orientation, it would be the person's attractions, and to exclude
this aspect is very problematic.[4]

An important reason why sexual behavior is an imperfect reflection of
one's true sexual desire and attractions is that sexual behavior often reflects a compromise between one's own inclinations and that of others. A
wife's sexual behavior (e.g., frequency of intercourse) reflects not only
her desires and inclinations but also her husband's, and vice versa. A
teenage boy's sexual behavior (frequency of masturbation, intercourse)
reflects his desires and inclinations as well as the availability of partners
and the social constraints imposed by his parents and peers.

As you might expect, behavior's imperfect reflection of one's desires
and attractions is also important in understanding asexuality. Sexual behavior—or more to the point, the absence of it—is usually not the defining feature of asexuality.[5] A more common definition, as mentioned, is a
lack of sexual attraction—or at least the definition in recent research often
includes this element (Bogaert, 2004; Bogaert, 2006b; Brotto et al., 2010).
Thus, although asexual people often have less sexual experience with a
partner, as one might expect, sexual experience per se would not necessarily mean that a person is not asexual (Bogaert, 2004). For example,
some asexual people may engage in partnered sex (e.g., sexual intercourse), perhaps out of curiosity or perhaps to please a romantic partner.
The latter type of sexual activity is most likely to occur in those asexuals
with romantic inclinations; it also reinforces the distinction made earlier
between romantic and sexual attraction.

It is also important to note that some people actively abstain from sex
for very long periods of time (e.g., prior to marriage, chastity), and some
people—celibates—actively eschew sex altogether, yet they do not necessarily lack sexual attraction. Indeed, they may be strongly sexually attracted to others but, for religious or other reasons, choose not to have

sex. For example, in Roman Catholic law and theology, "Clerics are obliged to observe perfect and perpetual continence for the sake of the kingdom of heaven and, therefore, are obliged to observe celibacy" (*Code of Canon Law*, n.d.). Such obligations, of course, are not always upheld in the long run. That celibacy in some forms of religious life is often so difficult to uphold attests to the fact that many celibates are not necessarily asexual. They may eventually stray and engage in some form of sexual behavior, because their sexual attractions and inclinations are so strong and overwhelm their values. That having been said, it is also not surprising that asexual people are, on average, more frequently found among the strongly religious (Bogaert, 2004). Celibacy is obviously much easier for those who are indeed asexual. A few years ago, a member of the clergy suggested to me that in his experience, asexuality was not unknown among those undertaking religious professions.

In 1980, Michael Storms recognized some of the limitations of a strictly behavioral approach to sexual orientation, including Kinsey's traditional behavioral scale for measuring sexual orientation. Thus, Storms's model of sexual orientation was based only on sexual attraction and not on actual behavior. He also argued that two seven-point scales/dimensions are better than one (Storms, 1980).

Storms's two scales or dimensions decouple homoeroticism (sexual attraction to the same sex) from heteroeroticism (sexual attraction to the opposite sex). So, if someone were asked on a questionnaire to categorize his or her sexual orientation using Storms's model, he or she would indicate the degree to which he or she has attractions to the same sex (homoeroticism) on a scale from low (one) to moderate (four) to high (seven), and then, on a separate scale, would indicate the degree to which he or she has attractions to the opposite sex (heteroeroticism), again ranging from low (one) to moderate (four) to high (seven). Having these two independent dimensions means that one can be high (or low) on one but also high (or low) on the other. Thus, one's score on one dimension does not constrain the score on the other. This means that one can be high on both (bisexuality) or low on both (asexuality). Storms never investigated asexuals to see if this model captures their attractions accurately (i.e., low on both dimensions), but, as mentioned above, there is now some support for this model (Bogaert, 2004; Brotto et al., 2010).

Now let's move on to the third letter of the alphabet, C. Recall that C is for *cognition*. *Cognition* is another word for "thoughts." For example, the field of cognitive psychology deals with the processing of information and knowledge. Thus, cognitive psychologists try to understand our thoughts and their organization in the mind; how, for example, one bit of knowledge or information is linked to another and how readily accessible this bit of knowledge is to our conscious mind.

Our thoughts are often organized into "knowledge structures" or "schemas." One form of knowledge structure is a script. A script is a cognitive generalization about the "appropriate sequence of events in a particular context" (Schank & Abelson, 1977, p. 41). In other words, just as a movie or a TV script tells an actor what to do and say (and when to do and say it), our cognitive scripts prompt us to do and say things in a specific order in a specific context. We may not realize that we carry around in our heads these cognitive "scripts" of what to do and say in various contexts, but we do. This type of cognitive processing is often automatic and unconsciously performed, and can provide very useful shortcuts for dealing with many contexts in the world around us. Indeed, it would be extremely time consuming and taxing if we had to deliberate about every move we make without relying on such mental shortcuts.

In sexual contexts, people also rely on scripts. Thus, humans engage in rather automated sequences of sexual behavior, dealing with behavioral contingencies in a rather orderly way (*First I will kiss her, then, if she responds to this, I will touch her breast, then I will . . .*). Of course, it takes time, it requires watching others perform these actions, and it takes practice (in keeping with the acting metaphor, let's call it *rehearsal*!) to make the sexual scripts unfold in a relatively seamless way, and sexual behavior is not without its complications, to say the least!

Sexual fantasies can be construed as a form of sexual script (see also chapter 5). Sexual fantasies may be very brief—just flashes of a sexy image bouncing around in our heads—but they can also be more elaborate, with a dramatic storyline or plot. If one has repeated fantasies, this may allow "rehearsal" to occur, so that we ingrain in our minds (potentially adaptive) sexual sequences of behavior—that is, sexual scripts.

Sexual fantasies, along with other cognitive processes, are important in understanding asexuality. For example, do asexual people have sexual fantasies or, if they are asexual but romantic, just romantic ones? If some asexual people do have sexual fantasies, what does this mean about their sexual attractions, given that sexual fantasies often closely reflect sexual attractions? Would such people truly lack sexual attraction?[6] We will be further discussing this issue and how other cognitive elements help us to understand sexuality and asexuality in various chapters (see, for instance, chapter 5 on masturbation and chapter 12 on humor).

D is for *desire*. Sexual desire can be defined as "a feeling that includes wanting to have a sexual experience, feeling receptive to a partner's sexual initiation, and thinking and fantasizing about sex" (Rosen et al., 2000, p. 191). *Desire* is another word for "lust," or, in more colloquial terms, "horniness"—that tingly feeling that makes people engage in sexual activity and, perhaps, have a release of sexual tension: orgasm.

Desire is related to all four of the above: attraction, arousal, behavior, and cognition. It is also, for example, very closely related to people's sexual attractions, as it usually is in reference to others. But desire and attraction also can be decoupled. One of the reasons for this decoupling is that there are separate bodily mechanisms underlying them. Circulating testosterone, for example, can have a large impact on desire, but it does not alter the direction of one's sexual attractions.[7] In the checkered early days of reparative therapy, gay men were administered high levels of testosterone, with the idea being that a lack of sexual interest in women occurred in men because of an insufficient amount of this male-associated hormone (Meyer-Bahlburg, 1977). The bottom line, however, was this: Testosterone did not make gay men heterosexual; it just made them horny! There were a couple of problems with this reparative approach using testosterone, aside from, of course, the ethical issues. First, testosterone, although found in higher concentrations in men than women, exists in both sexes. So, it is misleading to suggest that it is a *male-only* hormone (see also chapter 6). Second, prior to birth, different levels of exposure to testosterone may have permanent, organizing effects on the brain (as they do on the body), and may ultimately affect sexual attractions and one's orientation development (see also chapter 13). But in adolescence and adulthood, testosterone has "activating" effects, working like a kind of fuel on whatever disposition (i.e., brain organization) is already there in the first place. So it is not surprising that gay men, when given a boost of testosterone, became more interested in sexual activities generally but did not change their underlying attraction to men. So, in short, desire and attraction have different underlying bodily mechanisms, and hence are "decoupleable."

In many people's minds, asexual people must lack sexual desire (i.e., have no interest whatsoever in sexual activities). Indeed, very low desire or a lack of desire is sometimes put forth as an important definition of asexuality (Prause & Graham, 2007). I, too, think this definition of asexuality is a reasonable one, at least in some ways (Bogaert, 2006b; Bogaert, 2008). For example, I think lack of desire is more viable than lack of sexual behavior in defining asexuality.

But why I do prefer to define asexuality as a lack of sexual attraction (Bogaert, 2006b)? For one, if a person truly lacks sexual desire, then there is likely no sex drive to fuel any underlying sexual attractions, if indeed such underlying (perhaps) hidden attractions exist; thus, someone with an absence of desire would lack sexual attraction for others as well, although they still might have romantic attractions. Second, the reverse is not necessarily true: if one lacks sexual attraction, one does not necessarily have no sexual desire or drive (see chapter 5 on masturbation). Third, sexual attraction captures the core element of sexual orientation, so, if one wants to argue that asexual people do not have a traditional sexual orientation (i.e., gay, straight, bi) but instead have a unique *asexual* one, then a lack of sexual attraction to others is the important criterion (Bogaert, 2006b). Fourth, I think that a lack of desire may not capture accurately the phenomenon of asexuality, at least based on existing research. There is support for this view in two recent studies. Recent research on self-identified asexuals (Prause & Graham, 2007; Brotto et al., 2010) shows that they do not necessarily have a lower desire for sexual activity, but they clearly have a lower desire for sexual activity *with others*; in other words, they lack sexual attraction to others. Thus, a lack of sexual attraction is likely a good overarching definition of asexuality from a number of perspectives.[8]

This is not to say that someone who has had an enduring lack of desire for all forms of sexual activities, including partnered sex and masturbation, should not be labeled asexual. They should, in my view. This is because, as mentioned above, this person would lack sexual attraction for others (although perhaps not lack romantic attraction), along with lacking additional sexual processes (e.g., no sex drive). In fact, using an enduring lack of sexual desire for all sexual activities is, perhaps, a more stringent definition of asexuality than the one I have proposed, because it would include a lack of sexual attraction *and* a lack of sex drive. Thus, a lack of sexual attraction may be construed as a "minimal" definition for asexuality.

A couple of miscellaneous factors remain. One concerns sexual identity. Why not define an asexual person as anyone who, in fact, defines himself or herself as asexual? This is a reasonable question, and self-definitions/identities are important in a number of ways. For one, considering self-definitions respects the way someone chooses to label him or herself. There are also many interesting research and health issues about forging a sexual identity, including an asexual identity, as we will discuss in chapter 7. But is self-definition the best way to understand the main factor(s) underlying asexuality as a sexual orientation and/or as a phenomenon? Because one's sexual identity is often formed by a variety of factors—such as knowledge of a label or labels, comfort level with coming out, and political and other factors—many sexologists, including myself, are often wary of using self-identification as the key dimension in defining sexual orientation.[9] As mentioned above, many sexologists define sexual orientation in terms of sexual attraction, as we believe it is the "psychological core" of sexual orientation.

Another miscellaneous factor is pleasure. When we think of sex, we may think of sexual attractions, arousal, and desire, but we also think of pleasure. And when we do think of the pleasures of sex, we usually associate it with the arousal aspect (e.g., feelings of pleasure associated with erections and vaginal lubrication and the intense pleasure when physical arousal culminates in an orgasm). This makes sense because the organs of sex most directly associated with physical arousal (i.e., penis, clitoris, vagina) are brimming with nerve endings, which ultimately connect to the pleasure centers of the brain that are capable of making us experience intense pleasure. But all aspects of the sexual experience, broadly defined (including attraction, behavior, and desire), elicit a certain amount of pleasure. For example, a heterosexual man may experience pleasure at the mere sight of a beautiful woman (attraction) without ever—alas!—experiencing the physical pleasures (arousal/orgasm) of sex with her.

You may be thinking that this discussion on sexual pleasure is interesting, but also wondering, yet again, what all of this has to do with asexuality. Do asexual people lack sexual pleasure, and with all aspects of sex? It is likely the case that some asexual people may not have pleasure with many, if not all, aspects of sex, but a lack of pleasure does not seem to be the key defining factor associated with asexuality. Some asexual people do, for example, have arousal experiences and evidently receive pleasure from these experiences, as one of the quotes above, repeated here, demonstrates: "everything works fine, pleasurable and all, it's just not actually attracted to anything" (Brotto et al., 2010, p. 612). How many asexual people do nonetheless receive some level of pleasure from their arousal is unknown, but it is clear that a lack of sexual pleasure is not a defining feature for all asexual people.

SUMMARY

In this chapter we discussed the A (*attraction* and *arousal*), B (*behavior*), C (*cognition*), and Ds (*desire*) of sex. We also mentioned two miscellaneous factors: identity and pleasure. (I realize that by including I and P, I have ruined the alphabetical simplicity of my chapter title!) These are the key psychological processes of sexuality. They also help us to understand asexuality. Indeed, perhaps some asexual people are devoid of all these factors; that is, they lack sexual attraction, arousal, behavior, cognitions (e.g., fantasies), desire, and pleasure, and they also identify as "asexual." But one of these—lack of sexual attraction—may be a core psychological factor among asexual people and may best define the phenomenon, from both a theoretical and a research perspective. Lack of sexual attraction is at least potentially independent of these other processes, and it is noteworthy that those who lack sexual attraction may not lack these other processes (e.g., desire, arousal). Also, at this point, although lack of sexual attraction seems like a reasonable definition for understanding asexuality, the phenomenon is likely diverse, so it is important to keep in mind that this is a working definition and open to change. Thus, although I give some priority in this book, as I have in my past publications, to defining asexuality as a lack of sexual attraction, I think it is also reasonable to be sensitive to different definitions of asexuality (including a lack of desire for all sexual activities) and self-definitions. Another reason for being open to different definitions is that research on asexuality is just beginning.

NOTES

1. An interesting exception was pointed out to me when I was visiting a crocodile farm in Northern Territory, Australia. The caretakers noted a rare case of a male and female crocodile that seemed to have developed an affinity for one another and, unlike

all the other animals there, preferred to be caged together. They also slept on top of one another like love-obsessed newlyweds. Surprised that love would emerge in such an unnatural context, it made me wonder, a bit tongue in cheek, whether human love is partly a function of being in captivity.

2. For someone to be considered asexual, I think the lack of sexual attraction should have endured over a long period of time. For example, in my original study, a person was defined as asexual if he or she *never* had sexual attraction to others. Thus, like a heterosexual or homosexual orientation, which implies enduring level of attraction to others, there should be some level of persistence to one's lack of sexual attractions if one has an asexual orientation.

3. By the way, I call this "the drunk test." Armchair psychologists can use it to assess the deep-seated attractions, sexual and otherwise, of their friends, family, and acquaintances.

4. This is not to deny that there are times when we may not be able to know about a person's true inclinations and desires, because he or she may lie (or may not know) about them. Thus, if the behavior is "observable" in some way (e.g., getting caught with a prostitute), this may provide more accurate information than what people "report" on their attractions and desires. But this does not mean that if we had a faithful window into their minds, their attractions would be a worse indicator of who they are (as a sexual being) than their behaviors. Indeed, it would not. So, I reiterate: An accurate assessment of a person's attractions always trumps an accurate assessment of his or her behavior when it comes to understanding the true nature of that person's inclinations.

5. A recent exception to this is a study by Poston and Baumle (2010), which defined asexuality in a number of ways, including a lack of sexual behavior.

6. Indeed, sexual fantasies are so closely linked to one's sexual attractions that Storms's model of sexual orientation is sometimes referred to as the 2D *fantasy* model of sexual orientation (Storms, 1980).

7. I am using testosterone here as an example, but I don't want to imply that this hormone is the only factor at work. There are a number of factors other than testosterone—including psychosocial ones, for example—that influence sex drive.

8. That having been said, more research needs to be done on desire issues in asexual people. One issue that needs to be clarified is what asexual people mean by "no sexual desire" and "no sexual attraction," along with how they discriminate between these two aspects of sexuality. Most sexologists would likely indicate that desire refers to sex drive and interest, while sexual attraction refers to one's sexual inclination toward others. Most sexologists would also likely assert that there is a fair degree of overlap in what these two aspects capture about sexual expression for most people (Bogaert, 2006b). However, some (perhaps many) laypeople may use the terms "desire" and "attraction" differently than most sexologists do. For example, some people who identify as asexual may prefer to describe their asexuality as an issue of low/no desire, because they are more familiar with the word "desire," rather than "attraction," within the context of sexuality, and prefer the word "attraction" to describe romantic and affectionate orientations (and not necessarily a "sexual" inclination or orientation). Thus, these asexual people may have felt little "sexual" attraction for a partner of a particular gender (in the traditional sexual orientation sense), but still have strong romantic and affectionate attraction for these partners (see, for example, work by Lisa Diamond, 2003b). Consequently, they still describe their "attraction" for partners of a certain gender because of their romantic feelings/inclinations toward

them. Note: A similar point was made earlier in the chapter on romantic versus sexual attractions.

9. This is true especially if you consider the various names people use to describe their identity if they have same-sex attractions: gay, lesbian, queer, butch, femme, queen, and so forth.

THREE

History

The story of life begins asexually, and for most of Earth's natural history (about two-thirds of it), asexual reproduction has predominated (Cowen, 2005). It has only been in the last twelve hundred million years, out of the thirty-eight hundred million years that life has existed on Earth, that sexual reproduction has flourished—a mere fraction of geological time. Now it is the predominant form of reproduction for species on Earth.

The exact date of the emergence of sex—call it, ahem, the little bang theory—is a bit in question, however. Twelve hundred million years is a ballpark figure, give or take a few hundred million years. The first sex likely occurred in simple organisms, eukaryotes (Cowen, 2005). Eukaryotes are simple single- and multicell organisms, although they are more complex than the first single-cell organisms that predominated for about 2.5 billion years. Eukaryotes owe their complexity to sophisticated structures that the first forms of planetary life did not have, such as nuclei.

There are also other important dates in the evolution of sex beyond its first appearance. A second milestone in the natural history of sex was when this form of reproduction first occurred in the genealogical line leading to modern animals, perhaps about five hundred million years ago. This prize may belong to a worm-like creature called *Funisia*, the fossilized remains of which were originally found in Australia (Droser & Gehling, 2008). A third milestone was reached when the first "penetrative" sex appeared, around three hundred million years ago in a species of fish. These fossils were also originally found in Australia (Long, Trinajstic, & Johanson, 2009). Evidently, this fish's pelvic fin was used in pene-tration during copulation.

Note that not all sex involves penetration/copulation, as the definition of sexual reproduction is the combination of genetic material from two parents to form offspring. Sexual reproduction involves two processes: meiosis, the splitting in half of the parents' complement of genes, and fertilization, the recombination of genes by the melding of the parents' gametes (i.e., sperm and egg). Fertilization can be done in a variety of ways, one of which is internal, making penetration a common technique, but there are other ways of achieving this outcome.

It might be asked: If asexual reproduction was the way it all began, why is sex even here? This is an especially pertinent question, given that sex is a complex and costly way of reproducing one's genes. For example, there is considerable time and risk involved when it comes to finding a mate. Moreover, only 50 percent of an organism's (unique) genes are replicated in traditional sexual reproduction, versus 100 percent in asexu-al reproduction.

Although it is still debated, the most widely cited explanation for sexual reproduction concerns the creation of genetic variability, or the shuffling of the genes, which allows a species to survive in new and changing environments. This shuffling of genes may be particularly rele-vant for keeping ahead of various parasites that can take advantage of a gene pool lacking in diversity (Bell, 1982; Ridley, 1995; Van Valen, 1973). This explanation for the origin of sex is sometimes called the "Red Queen hypothesis," after the character in Lewis Carroll's *Through the Looking Glass* who exclaims, "It takes all the running you can do, to keep in the same place" (Carroll & Tenniel, 1960, p. 345). In other words, sex may have evolved as a weapon to win—but just barely so—the arms race against new environmental threats, including parasites.

This shuffling of genes may also be characterized as a type of "bet-hedging" strategy, allowing sexual reproducers to keep one step ahead of unknown threats in constantly new and changing environments. It is as if sexual reproducers are evolutionary dart players, throwing a variety of genetic arrows at the game board of life and seeing if one or more sticks.

The Red Queen hypothesis begs the question: If the shuffling of genes is often good for the health and vigor of organisms, why aren't there more than just *two* sexes? Surely a mating among more than two sexes would shuffle the genes even better than a mating between just two sexes. For example, why don't we see *tri*-sexual species—exotic characters belonging, seemingly, in a sci-fi movie—all over Earth? Well, actually, there are a number of species on Earth with three or more sexes (Roughgarden, 2004), but such examples are rare in Earth's natural history. Perhaps the costs associated with three or more sexes—such as having to find one another, and only reproducing a third of one's genes—is not sufficiently offset by the advantages of genetic diversity that combining three sexes would bring in producing offspring.

Most multicellular organisms are exclusively sexual reproducers. Yet there are spectacular exceptions to this rule, including some species larger than we are. Some sharks, for example, have the capacity to reproduce asexually. Scientists discovered this recently by accident when a female hammerhead shark in captivity in a zoo, without the company of any males, suddenly gave birth. It turned out that the mother hammerhead used a form of parthenogenesis, in which an unfertilized egg develops into an adult without any contribution from a male. The offspring in parthenogenesis is genetically identical to the mother and thus is always female. Subsequent biochemical analysis indicated that the offspring in the hammerhead case was genetically identical to the mother shark; thus, the scientists ruled out the possibility of stored sperm from a sneak fertilization with a male shark years earlier (Chapman et al., 2007; Eilperin, 2007, May 23). Talk about a virgin birth!

Humans are mammals, appearing relatively late on the planetary stage, so this ancient capacity to reproduce asexually still lingering in some very old (phylogenetically speaking) species does not exist in humans. Sharks have been around for a very long time, about 350 million years, as compared to humans (i.e., the genus *homo*), who have existed for—blink and you will miss it—a mere two to three million years.

There are also examples of seemingly exclusively asexual reproducers that, surprisingly, sometimes reproduce sexually. The fungus-farming ant, once thought to be an exclusively asexual reproducer (indeed, the species consists of all females), has been found to have telltale signs of sexual reproduction: some of the offspring were not 100 percent identical to the queen in one of the subpopulations of these ants, and the queen herself had—aha!—storage organs in her body that were filled with sperm (Rabeling et al., 2011; Ghose, 2011, July 18). These authors argue that sexual reproduction in this subpopulation may provide certain advantages (e.g., the ability to extend its range to new and complex environments) over those exclusively asexual subpopulations of ants. Relatedly, the authors argue that such glimpses of sexual reproduction in normally asexual species may provide an important view of how the evolution of sexuality occurs: "If you come back in five million or ten million years, there's a good chance the asexual lineages go extinct, but the sexual lineages are still existing" (Ghose, 2011, July 18).

The above brief discussion of the natural history of asexual and sexual reproduction only indirectly relates to the main subject of this book: asexual humans. The *type* of reproduction of a species—sexual or asexual—is somewhat different from the phenomenon of asexual beings, including human beings, *within* an exclusively sexually reproducing species. There is also a distinction between sexuality and the capacity for reproduction. For example, the vast majority of asexual people can still reproduce sexually (i.e., are still part of the sexually reproducing species of humans), even if they are not interested in the sexual mechanisms of it. Finally, in modern humans, sexuality is often divorced from reproduction, so asexuality is (partially) a different phenomenon than asexual reproduction.

More to the main point of this book, then, are there examples of asexual animals within a normally sexually reproducing species? There are. For example, a chorus line of sexual variability exists in farm and lab animals, even though they are often bred—and sometimes genetically altered—to be nearly identical food-producing or lab-friendly machines. As in humans, you can find some that are studs or sexual dynamos. You can also find some having "homosexual" tendencies, in that they prefer sexual relations with the same sex; for example, males not only affiliating with other males but also actively preferring to mount other males rather than females. You can also find animals that have no sexual interest whatsoever in other animals. This pattern of sexual variation among animals is often most clearly observed in males, as it is sometimes harder to determine female sexual tendencies, in part because they, relative to males, are less likely to initiate mating, often having a more subtle sexual response associated with receptivity (see chapter 6 on gender).

Male rodents raised in experimental labs (e.g., mice, gerbils, guinea pigs) often demonstrate wide sexual variability, with behaviors ranging from hypersexual to asexual. These extremes are often called "studs" and "duds," respectively. Such variability in rodents may have parallels to human sexual variability, including asexuality. Yet there are a number of unknowns. First, some non-mating males may have sexual attraction to other males, and so a lack of mating may not mean asexuality. A second, related unknown is that the conclusions rely on the *behavior* of the animals, and this is an imperfect measure of underlying sexual attractions, particularly if we are using it as a model of human sexual attractions (see also chapter 2). Third, researchers are unclear as to what factor(s), biological or otherwise, underlie the stud/dud difference. One biological explanation is variations in circulating testosterone, as this hormone is related to sex drive in both animals and humans. However, some animal experiments, including early ones on guinea pigs, indicate that variations in adult-level circulating hormones are probably not the main cause of the difference between duds and studs, because these animals, after being castrated and then readministered a constant level of testosterone, still showed the same behavioral differences (Grunt & Young, 1952; Adkins-Reagan, 2005). Another possibility is that there are differences in certain brain cell structures laid down before birth—called receptors—that make some animals more or less sensitive to testosterone exposure in adulthood. A related possibility is that prenatal hormones organize certain sites of the brain into groupings of cells (nuclei) with specialized functions. This difference in how brain cells are organized/structured prior to birth has implications for human sexual orientation, as a leading biological theory of human sexual orientation proposes that similar mechanisms underlie human variations in sexual attraction. Thus, from a sexual orientation perspective, these "dud" animals may have an asexual orientation because of prenatal factors organizing the brain in a certain way, just as variations in human sexual attractions, including perhaps asexuality, may be affected by such prenatal influences.

Did you know that there are sexual-orientation "tests" in male sheep (rams)? And no, I do not mean measures of genital responding while the rams view pictures of sheep, or even a "drunk test" (see chapter 2). In the United States Sheep Experiment Station in Dubois, Idaho, researchers test the erotic inclinations of their animals by allowing rams to have access to two "stimulus" females (ewes) in estrus or to two "stimulus" rams. These sexual-orientation tests occur in specialized pens, over repeated time periods (e.g., three thirty-minute exposures). The stimulus animals are restrained, so the test rams have easy access to them. The rams' sexual interest is measured by observing various mating behaviors characteristic of these animals: sniffs, kicks, mounting attempts, and "flehmans" (i.e., head raisings with curling of the upper lip) (Roselli, Larkin, Schrunk, & Stormshak, 2004).

But why would researchers test rams for their erotic inclinations in the first place? They do so to understand and ultimately increase the productivity of rams for sheep farmers, who want, as you might expect, stud rams to produce lots of little lambs.

If the rams are sexually attracted to ewes, they are called FORs (female-oriented rams); if they are attracted to other rams, they are called MORs (male-oriented rams). If they are attracted to neither, they are called NORs (no-oriented rams), or asexuals.

A surprisingly high percentage are MORs, but equally surprising is that a high percentage are evidently NORs (i.e., asexual). For example, here is a quote by researchers Charles Roselli and colleagues in a paper summarizing their results: "Over the past 2 years, 584 rams were tested. Of these 12.5% were asexual, 55.6% mounted and attained ejaculation with ewes, 9.5% mounted other rams, and 22% interacted sexually with both males and females" (Roselli et al., 2004, p. 235).

As in rodents, there does not seem to be strong evidence that sexual variation among the rams is related to circulating testosterone. For example, asexual rams (NORs) do not have lower levels of testosterone than the FORS or the MORs (Perkins, Fitzgerald, & Price, 1992), also suggesting that asexual rams may develop their sexual orientation because of prenatal factors organizing the brain in a certain way.

Rams may be especially relevant to understanding human sexuality; indeed, they provide a better animal comparison to human sexual orientation than male rodents, because rams show similar patterns of sexual behavior to human males. For example, MORs actively pursue other males for sexual liaisons, as do human men sexually interested in other men. Thus, sexual orientation patterns in both species, perhaps including asexuality, may emerge because of similar prenatal mechanisms, such as exposure to prenatal hormones organizing sites of the brain (see chapter 13). Indeed, research suggests that structural differences in a site of the lower brain, the SDN-POA (sexually dimorphic nucleus of the preoptic area) of the hypothalamus, is relevant to ram sexual orientation, just as a similar site is likely relevant to men's sexual orientation (Roselli, Stormshak, Stellflug, & Resko, 2002; LeVay, 1991). However, the researchers have not as yet examined the brains of NORs to determine if this site is related to asexual rams' sexual orientation.

A final note on these animal studies: They are interesting and well worth considering as they relate to human asexuality, but recall the caution about animal behavior being an imperfect model of underlying attractions, particularly as they apply to human sexual attractions (see also chapter 2 on the attraction/behavior distinction).

Let's move from natural history to human history. Many humans throughout history have lived their lives without sex.[1] A reality of human life, from the emergence of human beings to their existence in the present day, is that some people, even when motivated, do not find mates. These people may have had certain traits—very low physical attractiveness, extreme shyness, or other factors—that made finding a partner difficult. So, a lack of (partnered) sexual behavior is sometimes not a matter of choice.

Sometimes a lack of (partnered) sexual behavior has less to do with the characteristics of the individual per se and more to with the fact that abstinence is thrust upon them. Elizabeth Abbott, in her book *The History of Celibacy* (2001), gives a number of examples of this type of imposed abstinence. Ming emperors in China, for example, sometimes had young males in the court castrated. This rather harsh physical change was meant to encourage loyal service and discourage hanky-panky with the emperors' wives and courtesans. Similarly, in the royal courts of ancient Rome and Europe, castration of males was not unknown. This procedure probably did reduce the sexual behavior of those subjected to it, as the testicles are the major source of the major sex-drive hormone, testosterone. It also effectively maintained the sweet-sounding voices of some of the top choirboys, who sang to please the upper classes, including royalty, in Europe. However, these *castrati* also attest to the fact that (testicular) testosterone is not the only influence on sexual behavior, as some of these castrated men seemed to be sexual, even several years after the procedure (Heriot, 1956).

A lack of sexual behavior based on one's own choice has also been a historical reality. That this is so reflects the value that many societies and institutions, often religious in nature, have placed on abstinence. Celibacy or chastity has been a standard vow in many religiously devoted people—priests, monks, and nuns—for many years. And, of course, even today many contemporary clergy and other religiously devoted individuals still adopt a celibate lifestyle.

Many celibates do not lack sexual attraction or a sex drive, and thus are not asexual using the most common definitions of asexuality. So, we can now pose the question that is more relevant to the subject of this book: Is there good evidence of asexuality in the historical record? This is a difficult question, because human sexual behavior (or the lack of it), like animal sexual behavior, is more easily measured and recorded than are (internal) psychological states, such as attractions or desires. Except for having access to, say, love letters and diaries, such inner states are often hidden, or at least under the radar, and certainly not routinely recorded in the history books.

Even so, one's attractions and desires may be inferred, albeit imperfectly, from behavior. If the historical record suggests that a man had a wife and numerous children, and that he had liaisons with prostitutes, and along with these liaisons a number of illegitimate children, it is very likely that he was heterosexual. In contrast, if the man shunned the institution of marriage, had no children, and there is little evidence of any liaisons with either sex, we could infer one of two things: either the individual was attracted to the same sex, and thus hid potentially socially undesirable sexual behavior, or he was perhaps sexually attracted to neither sex.

Based largely on reports of their behavior, it may be surmised that a number of famous figures throughout history, Isaac Newton and Emily Brontë among them, were asexual. Newton, for example, never married, lived a solitary life, likely died a virgin, and seemed completely preoccupied with his science (Christianson, 1984). Although evidence of a lack of sexual behavior with women suggests that Newton was asexual, such evidence may also be construed to mean that he had other atypical sexual inclinations (e.g., same-sex attraction). Indeed, some have suggested Newton eschewed the company of women because he was sexually attracted to men (White, 1999).

Emily Brontë also very likely lived a life devoid of sexual liaisons; indeed, she also probably died a virgin. However, if she was asexual, she likely was not aromantic (see chapter 2 for distinction between sex and romance), or at least she had a high-level understanding of romance, as she wrote one of the most intensely romantic novels of her time, *Wuthering Heights*. Thus, did she eschew the company of men for sexual reasons, but not necessarily for romantic reasons? Or did she perhaps have a special insight into the world of romance because she was an outsider (asexual/aromantic), as well as a keen observer of humanity? The novelist Stevie Davies (2004) argues that Brontë may have been sexual in some form (e.g., masturbated), and may have had sexual attraction, but this was not overtly expressed in her lifetime because it was directed toward women. Of course, as is the case with Newton, the assertion that Brontë had an atypical sexual orientation, either an asexual or same-sex one, is based on limited evidence.

It is interesting to speculate on whether some individuals who may have been asexual in the past—that is, experiencing no sexual attraction or no desire for any sexual activity—may have been sexual if they had lived in contemporary Western society. This assumes of course that environmental and cultural factors play some role in sexualizing individuals (see chapter 13), and that these factors are (more) prevalent in modern Western society relative to other time periods and societies. For example, there is some evidence that, at least up until recently, there may have been more asexuals, broadly defined, in China than in the West (see chapter 4), and that this may reflect more restrictive sexual norms in that society. Thus, could the social environment of the Victorian era in England have contributed to Emily Brontë's asexuality (if she was in fact asexual)? And if so, had she lived in modern Western society, and was exposed in childhood and adolescence to its sexualizing influences, such as Lady Gaga videos, would she have developed into a sexual person? Of course, we also have to recognize that some people with strong predispositions to be asexual, because of the prenatal influences mentioned above, may be immune to such forces. But it is worth considering how cultural forces, as they have changed over time, can contribute to the sexualization, or the lack of it, of individuals.

As we move into very recent history, the evidence for the existence of asexual people becomes more solid. This is because the modern age of communication provides a rich source of information on people's lives, including recordings of individuals talking candidly about their sexual feelings.

Paul Erdos, one of the most famous mathematicians of recent history, was asexual (NNDB.com, 2011). Like Newton, he was profoundly preoccupied with his science. One of his biographies is aptly named *The Man Who Loved Only Numbers* (Hoffman, 1998). Erdos spoke about how deeply moved he was by mathematics, and his aesthetic appreciation of it over all other things, including (presumably) people: "If numbers aren't beautiful, I don't know what is" (Schechter, 1998, p. 7). He also spoke about his lack of sexual interest: "I can't stand sexual pleasure" (Csicsery, 1993). It is not known whether this statement refers to a general disinterest in all aspects of sexuality—attraction, desire, arousal—or just the arousal/ pleasure component, but it is clear that Erdos did not seek out the intimate company of others. Moreover, given that his aesthetic interests seemed primarily limited to mathematics, he likely did not have a deep sexual (or even romantic) attraction to other people (see also chapter 12).

Throughout history, artists have produced figures in paintings and sculptures and portrayed characters in fiction that project an asexual aura. Not only do such depictions reflect the artist's sensitivity to existing human variability—a variability that the audience can understand and respond to—but they also serve two dramatic functions: first, to emphasize a value that the artist or his or her patron holds dear, and second, to increase the conflict or tension that makes storytelling work.

As an example of the former, an asexual portrayal may serve to reinforce the notion that a character is immune to worldly temptations, or perhaps is completely consumed or driven by one goal and motive. So, the portrayal of a character may de-emphasize secondary sex characteristics (e.g., women's breasts), or perhaps present them in an androgynous manner. The Virgin Mary, saints, and angels have often been portrayed in this way throughout the history of European Christian art.

It was also for this reason that Arthur Conan Doyle gave his fictional character, Sherlock Holmes, an asexual aura: to portray his character as being driven by intellect. Interest in the flesh could potentially compromise Holmes's power of reasoning. Indeed, Holmes is presented as being above (or somewhat immune to) most other pleasures of the body, including eating. In Watson's words: "It was one of his peculiarities that in his more intense moments he would permit himself no food, and I have known him to presume upon his iron strength until he has fainted from pure inanition" (Doyle, 2003, p. 32).

The second reason for portraying asexual characters—to increase tension and conflict in drama—is something artists (particularly writers) understand implicitly, as character is often a driving force in storytelling. Indeed, theorists of fiction have pointed out the important role of character in effective storytelling (Morrell, 2006), and human variability (sexual and otherwise) is the raw material for the development and portrayal of character.

Note that I am not merely referring to high art here. Examples of asexual characters (or characters who have an asexual aura) help drive fiction in the popular media, with some of it, of course, far from being considered high art. Indeed, perhaps the most important examples are ones found in the popular media, as those venues have a wide appeal to psychological and social forces common to most, if not all, people.

A prime example of asexuals in low art is the title character in the TV program *Gilligan's Island*. This program ran for three years in the late 1960s, but the relatively short stint on TV belies the popularity of this program, as it was very successful in reruns for many years. Thus, it had a large appeal, at least for a segment of the population. Other than the title character, Gilligan, the male characters on this TV program—the Skipper, the Professor, and even Mr. Howell—projected an asexual aura at times, but Gilligan was essentially asexual. Although physically mature, he evinced little sexual desire or attraction.

Why was he portrayed so? The simple answer, I believe, is the writers knew that this type of character portrayal had appeal for preadolescent boys—indeed, a large portion of the audience for this program may have been boys—who could identify with Gilligan, in part because of their own asexuality or, more accurately, presexuality. A sexual Gilligan would not have appealed to their sensibilities, and perhaps even threatened them. Also, his asexuality made good fodder for the type of humor in which this show reveled: One of the female characters, the movie star Ginger, was very sexual, at least for that time in TV-land, and thus her overtures to Gilligan made for comedic tension.

Today there is a character on TV who is Gilligan's sexual equal: Sheldon, from the popular show *The Big Bang Theory*. He is, of course, Gilligan's intellectual superior by light years, an academic nerd of epic proportions, but the humor of this show partly derives from a similar dramatic/comedic tension: the character's asexuality brushing up against a sexual world.

Another character with an asexual aura who predates Gilligan and also may outlive Sheldon is Jughead Jones, Archie's male sidekick in the popular comic series created in the 1940s. Jughead is consumed with interests (hamburgers, mostly) other than the usual teenage preoccupation of finding and keeping mates. In the modern incarnation of this series, there has been a suggestion that Jughead is gay—for instance, a male character "comes out" to him (IBNLive.com, 2011, April 2)—but I expect that the original writers wanted Jughead presented asexually. Thus, although the "asexual" word likely did not creep into the writers' editorial meetings (at least those in the early years), Jughead was likely created as an asexual (and aromantic) contrast to Archie, who was girl crazy.

As mentioned, women have also often been portrayed in art and the popular media as asexual—for example, the iconic virgin. Such icons are presented in high art (e.g., religiously inspired art of the Virgin Mary) to highlight virtues, but also in more popular fiction to increase tension and drama. For example, iconic asexual female characters seem to occur with regular frequency in dramas or comedies—perhaps a naïve ingénue or a nerdy, priggish librarian (complete with thick glasses). These portrayals may enhance the dramatic/comedic arc of a story, because these asexual female characters may likewise brush up against a sexual world. They also offer a glimpse, or at least a fantasy, of an asexual character possibly becoming sexualized. No doubt such glimpses, if they are realized, have a titillating appeal to some heterosexual male audiences.

That asexual characters seem to be of a "type" or routinely have certain characteristics—such as the asexual "man-child" (Gilligan), the intellectual nerd (Sheldon), the asexual prig (the librarian)—may speak to our expectations of how asexuality often manifests itself in people in the real world, even if these expectations are often distorted stereotypes.

The history of asexuality should also include some mention of the emergence of asexual identities. As discussed in chapter 6, the identification as an asexual person ("I am asexual") is probably a recent phenomenon, and largely a Western one at that.[2] Use of the word "asexual" to describe an individual may also be a relatively modern, Western phenomenon. This modern use of the term likely emerged from an increased public awareness of asexuality in response to recent media attention to one of my asexuality papers and a popular scientific paper on asexuality by Sylvia Pagan Westphal, both of which appeared in 2004 (Bogaert, 2004; Westphal, 2004). It also occurred because of David Jay, who is, speaking of history, an important figure in the modern story of asexuality. He is an asexual man, the founder of the Asexual Visibility and Education Network (AVEN), and he has been assertive in promoting awareness of asexuality.

It is unclear exactly how many people in the modern world identify as asexual (see chapter 10), but the emergence of this term, and an asexual identity in general, probably fills an important psychological void for a number of people not comfortable with traditional categories of sexual identities (CNN.com, 2004).

SUMMARY

One of this book's themes is that the study of asexuality informs the study of sexuality. At a basic biological level, this is true: The study of asexual species and their adaptability—or lack of it—in changing environments gives clues as to why sexuality exists. Within a sexual species, asexual variation also informs sexuality. For example, sexuality researchers are finding some evidence that the potential mechanisms—such as prenatal hormones organizing brain sites—underlying an asexual orientation are the same as those underlying traditional sexual orientations (i.e., gay versus straight). It is certain that many humans never mated throughout history, but it is unclear how many people were asexual— that is, lacked sexual attraction or desire—for much of human history. In recent times, however, evidence of asexuality is clear. Asexuality has also been portrayed throughout the history of art. That humans create asexual figures and characters attests to a common understanding that sexual variation exists, and that sexuality, at least in art, sometimes needs a dramatic foil.

NOTES

1. Of course, some of these people may have never masturbated, if one wants to define sexuality broadly, beyond sexual activities with a partner.
2. A case in point: in the 1960s, I doubt viewers would likely have identified Gilligan as an "asexual."

FOUR

The Prevalence of Asexuality

As if! I do not know if anyone has actually said those exact words to me. If not, they should have, because they capture the reaction I have gotten from some people when I have told them the prevalence rate of asexuality (1 percent), based on my first published study of asexuality in 2004 (Bogaert, 2004). In short, some people's reaction has been one of disbelief (Fulbright, 2009, January 12), questioning that as many as 1 percent or more of human beings could be asexual. Frankly, I think that some people would question that *anyone* could be truly asexual, even if I had reported the rate at .00001 percent.

The 1 percent figure is intriguing, I must admit, perhaps if only because it is a memorably round number. Such round numbers, be they large or small, do seem to have a capacity to intrigue and stimulate debate, if not to polarize. Indeed, I think one of the reasons why I was drawn to publishing these data on asexuality was because this nice round number did, in fact, intrigue me. *Hmmm*, I thought. *Could this figure be correct? Could it be true that such a mighty minority has been overlooked on the sexual landscape? Could it even be that 1 percent is an underestimate?*

This figure is also likely one of the reasons why the media chose to publicize the asexuality story, or perhaps the reason why the story "had legs." It is a good headline that reads, "Study: 1 in 100 adults asexual" (CNN.com, 2004, October 14).

In this chapter, I discuss the prevalence of asexuality. What exactly is the correct figure, and why does it matter? I also explore this "As if!" reaction. Specifically, why do some people have this reaction, and what does it reveal about the way we think and about our culture? In other words, what conclusions can be drawn about the human psyche and our society if some people do not believe that there could be a small group of people who are so different from them, sexually speaking?

Traditionally, prevalence research in the sexual orientation field has centered on gays and lesbians, who constitute a more visible and well-known sexual minority than asexual people. Most early estimates of same-sex sexuality were loosely based on data collected by Alfred Kinsey, the pioneer sex researcher, who, along with his colleagues, interviewed thousands of Americans from the 1930s through the 1950s (Kinsey, Pomeroy, & Martin, 1948; Kinsey, Pomeroy, Martin, & Gebhard, 1953). The most widely cited estimate of same-sex sexuality that was loosely based on this work was 10 percent (Marmor, 1980; Voeller, 1990). Note that this 10 percent figure was only "loosely based" on Kinsey's work, because it actually only referred to the percentage of men (and not women) in his original sample who had reported predominantly same-sex activity, and Kinsey himself never claimed that 10 percent of Americans were gay.

Like 1 percent, a 10 percent figure is a memorably round number that draws people in. Thus, it also has "had legs." Over the years, gay and lesbian people have used a somewhat cheeky and/or subversive code[1] to identify themselves (e.g., "queer," "bent," "friends of Dorothy"), and, not surprisingly, some have chosen to rally around this 10 percent figure. For example, some gay people claim proudly to be a member of the "Ten Percent" club or society (Hecox, n.d.). There are also postmodern, consumer riffs on this figure and its meaning for gay and lesbian people, in which, for example, shopping online in gay-friendly establishments allows one to snag a 10 percent discount (10percent.com, n.d.).

Yet Kinsey's sample, although useful even today for a number of different purposes, was never a good one to use for estimating prevalence rates of sexual behavior (or the people who engage in it). It was not representative of the United States and skewed to include a high percentage of sexual minorities, in which Kinsey had a special interest. Thus, the 10 percent figure is questionable, because it is based on an unrepresentative, although very historically significant, sample of the U.S. population.

The AIDS era (i.e., post-1985) is not a high point in the history of human sexuality, because of its effects on sexual minorities, but it did usher in the age of good sampling methods to study sexuality. These

new, modern samples usually recruit people nationwide and are generally representative of the populations they survey. One form of modern
survey research utilizes national probability sampling. This procedure
selects people randomly from the population but also tries to ensure that
different subgroups of a nation's population (e.g., regions, ethnicities)
have an equal or a "known" probability of being chosen, even if they are
harder to sample for some reason (e.g., a population that is more remote,
or difficult to contact by phone). For example, if Asian women comprise 5
percent of a nation's population, then 5 percent of the sample should
contain Asian women. As we will see later, these modern, nationwide
probability samples are not perfect, particularly as the reality of sampling
is different than the theory of sampling, but they are much better than the
majority of other samples used in research. The majority of research samples are called "convenience" samples, because the participants are recruited at the researcher's convenience (people who happen to respond
to a recruitment ad in a magazine, an undergraduate class that a professor recruits for a study she is conducting, etc.). These convenience samples are certainly useful at times, but they do not represent the broader
population.

Using modern, nationwide probability samples, researchers have
found that the prevalence of both male and female homosexuality is lower than the 10 percent figure. The estimate based on one of the best U.S.
samples, the National Health and Social Life Survey, is that gay and
lesbian people make up about 2–3 percent of the population (Laumann,
Gagnon, Michael, & Michaels, 1994). Other samples, including in other
Western countries, have also suggested lower figures than 10 percent
(Billy, Tanfer, Grady, & Klepinger, 1993; Sell, Wells, & Wypij, 1995; Joloza, Evans, & O'Brien, 2010). For example, using the Integrated Household
Survey, researchers found that 1.5 percent of 238,206 British residents
identified as lesbian, gay, or bisexual (Joloza et al., 2010). The author of a
recent book on sexual orientation, biologist Simon LeVay, after reviewing
the available data, suggests that approximately 2–5 percent of men and
approximately 1–2 percent of women are predominantly or exclusively
homosexual (LeVay, 2010).

Although they are the best data available, these modern prevalence
figures of same-sex sexuality come with a few caveats. First, they are
largely, but not exclusively, based on same-sex behavior or on having a
same-sex identity. Yet how should we best define homosexuality: as

same-sex behavior, as *a same-sex identity*, as *same-sex attraction*, or as perhaps all three? As discussed earlier, in chapter 2, many sex researchers, including me, place a high value on attraction over overt behavior (or even identity) in defining a traditional sexual orientation (Bailey, Dunne, & Martin, 2000; Bogaert, 2003; Money, 1988; Zucker & Bradley, 1995). I continue this emphasis on attraction in the present book on asexuality. I do so because sexual attraction is, in my opinion, the "core" psychological element of sexual orientation; it is less changeable and less subject to influence by social and political conditions than one's behavior or how one chooses to define oneself. Based on same-sex attraction figures alone, the estimates tend to be slightly lower than, for example, those based on behavior: about 2 percent of men and 1 percent of women are predominantly or exclusively gay/lesbian (Laumann et al., 1994).

A second caveat is that there is still stigma about admitting to same-sex sexuality, so even if these modern samples represent their populations well, these figures likely underestimate the prevalence of homosexuality. Third, non-Western societies are not considered in these figures, and it is important to remember that the majority of the people in the world do not live in Western societies, although most people in Western societies behave as if they do. For example, I do not know of a good estimate of homosexuality in India, Russia, Iran, or countless other non-Western societies. A recent exception is China. The estimate of same-sex sexuality in China is lower than estimates for most Western countries, with, for example, approximately 1 percent of men and women indicating that they identify as homosexual. The question was: "Some people regard themselves as homosexual. Do you so regard yourself?" (Parish et al., 2003; Parish, Das, & Laumann, 2006; Parish, Luo, Laumann, Kew, & Yu, 2007). Slightly fewer, just less than 1 percent, indicated that they had sexual attraction for (i.e., wanted to have sex with) the same sex. The stigma associated with same-sex attraction is likely high, so one expects that these figures are underestimating same-sex sexuality, even more so than in Western societies. However, even factoring in this underestimate, I expect that it is unlikely that predominant or exclusive same-sex sexuality would reach the memorably round 10 percent figure in either Western or non-Western societies.

Why is this prevalence research on homosexuality important for understanding the prevalence rate of asexuality? It is important because it allows a broad context to understand the prevalence rate of asexuality and, more specifically, provides a comparison to another sexual minority.

Given our discussion of Kinsey, we should give a nod to his data before we discuss modern samples and their evidence for the prevalence of asexuality. As you may recall, Kinsey called asexual (or nonsexual) people Xs, because they did not conveniently correspond to a number on his seven-point scale of sexual orientation. Kinsey tallied his numbers for Xs, just as he did for people with traditional sexual orientations. In the male sample, 1.5 percent were Xs (Kinsey et al., 1948). In his female sample (Kinsey et al., 1953), he reported different rates of Xs depending on their marital status. For example, 14–19 percent of unmarried women were Xs, whereas 1–3 percent of married women were Xs.[2]

In the post-AIDs era of good sampling, few social scientists would dare to make estimates on asexuality without resorting to findings in national surveys with modern sampling methods (e.g., probability sampling), such as the one I will use here. As mentioned, in the first published study using a British national sample, the National Survey of Sexual Attitudes and Lifestyles (NATSAL-I) (Johnson, Wadsworth, Wellings, & Field, 1994), I found that 1.05 percent of the population reported that they had "never felt sexual attraction to anyone at all." This rate was very similar to the prevalence rate of same-sex attraction (i.e., predominant homosexuality and bisexuality combined) in this survey, which was 1.1 percent (Bogaert, 2004).

Intriguing as this 1 percent figure is, it does not necessarily represent a definitive statement on the prevalence of asexuality across societies, or even across time within the same society. I recently reanalyzed the ten-year follow-up to this national British sample (NATSAL-II) (Johnson et al., 2001; National Centre for Social Research et al., 2005), and found that approximately 0.5 percent had "never felt sexual attraction to anyone at all" (Bogaert, in press-a). Also, as a comparison, the prevalence rate of same-sex attraction (again, predominant homosexuality and bisexuality combined) was higher in NATSAL-II (2.3 percent) than in NATSAL-I and was significantly higher than the rate of asexuality in NATSAL-II.

Why the difference in prevalence rates of asexuality and homosexuality between these two national British samples? The difference likely occurred because the two samples varied in meaningful ways (Johnson et al., 2001). First, only sixteen- to forty-four-year-olds were recruited for NATSAL-II, whereas NATSAL-I had a broader range of ages, sixteen to fifty-nine. In my original study, I found that asexual people were more likely to be older rather than younger. Thus, the prevalence of asexuality may have been lower in NATSAL-II because it contained a restricted age range. Second, NATSAL-II participants, relative to NATSAL-I participants, may have been somewhat more sexually liberal in a variety of dimensions (e.g., attitudes, interests, and behavior). Thus, asexual people—who have, for example, less sexual experience relative to sexual people—may have been less extensively recruited to participate in NATSAL-II relative to NATSAL-I. Similarly, people with more liberal sexual attitudes and behavior, including gays and lesbians (who often have more sexual experience and are more liberal), may have been more extensively recruited in NATSAL-II relative to NATSAL-I. But is there evidence that NATSAL-II indeed surveyed more sexually liberal people than NATSAL-I? Yes, there is some. First, there was a ten-year span between recruitments for NATSAL-I and NATSAL-II, and sexual attitudes and behaviors often change across time, and usually in the more liberal direction. Second, there was a more extensive survey of greater London in NATSAL-II relative to NATSAL-I (see National Centre for Social Research et al., 2005), and urban people are often more liberal and sexually experienced relative to more rural people. However, the researchers did attempt to account for the greater recruitment of Londoners in NATSAL-II versus NATSAL-I using statistical methods (Bogaert, in press-a). Another consideration is that the method of assessment in NATSAL-II was likely more private than in NATSAL-I, and thus NATSAL-II participants may have been potentially more open to revealing sensitive information (e.g., same-sex attraction) (Copas et al., 2002).

How about societies beyond Britain? There is a representative sample of Australia with relevant information on sexual attraction, the Australian Study of Health and Relationships (ASHR). Like NATSAL-I, the ages surveyed were sixteen to fifty-nine, and the sexual orientation question allowed for the response "I never felt sexual attraction to anyone at all." Approximately 0.4 percent reported never having felt sexual attraction to others, as compared to the 2 percent rate of same-sex attraction in this sample (again, same-sex and bisexual attraction combined) (Smith, Rissel, Richters, Grulich, & de Visser, 2003).

In addition to the NATSAL studies in Britain and this national sample of Australia, there are important data on sexual attraction (or the lack of it) in the U.S.-based National Survey of Family Growth (NSFG) (Mosher,

Chandra, & Jones, 2005; Poston & Baumle, 2010), also a national sample. When asked about their sexual attractions (to men, women, or both), 0.8 percent of female participants and 0.7 percent of male participants reported that they were "not sure." This is in contrast to 1.5 percent of female participants who reported predominant or exclusive attraction to women and 1.9 percent who reported equal sexual attraction to both sexes, and also in contrast to 2.2 percent of male participants who reported predominant or exclusive attraction to men and 1 percent who reported equal sexual attraction to both sexes. Assuming that "not sure" is a reasonable proxy for a lack of sexual attraction, these figures should be considered as "in-between" the prevalence rate of asexuality that I reported in the NATSAL samples (Bogaert, 2004; Bogaert, in press-a). However, "not sure" is a vague answer and could mean, at least for some, something beyond a lack of sexual attraction for others. Also, like NATSAL-II, the age range was restricted in NSFG, in this case to only those between fifteen and forty-four.

Some national surveys have also included information on low or absent sexual desire. Low or absent desire is not completely overlapping with a lack of sexual attraction—my preferred definition of asexuality— but it is clearly related, particularly in the case of absent desire, and may serve as a good proxy for lack of sexual attraction, especially when no specific information was collected on sexual attraction. Moreover, the absence of desire is an alternative way to define asexuality (see chapter 2 on definitions of asexuality) (Prause & Graham, 2007). Thus, figures on low/absent desire should also give us pause about the true number of "asexuals," broadly defined. Using a national survey of Danish residents, Soren Ventegodt (1998) found that 11.2 percent of women and 3.2 percent of men had "low sexual desire." In one of the best sex survey samples from the United States, the National Health and Social Life Survey (NHSLS), Laumann and colleagues found that approximately one-third of women and one-seventh of men had "low desire" in the past year (Laumann, Paik, & Rosen, 1999). In a recent national sample of China, 7 percent of participants reported "no" desire for a year or more (Parish et al., 2003; Parish et al., 2006; Parish et al., 2007; Bogaert, 2008).

Although these studies are interesting, it should be noted that in two of the studies (those by Ventegodt and Laumann and his colleagues), low desire is not necessarily the same as absence of desire. Also, it is important to consider the time frame in these studies, as it is unclear whether these individuals would report low or even absent desire over many years. I think it is reasonable, after all, to define asexuality as a relatively long-term, or stable, characteristic (see chapter 2 on definitions).

There has never been a national survey assessing an asexual "identity." However, there are intriguing sexual identification data from the U.S.-based National Survey of Family Growth, mentioned above (Mosher et al., 2005; Poston & Baumle, 2010). Like in many large-scale surveys, the respondents were asked to define their sexual orientation. In addition to the option of endorsing one of the three traditional categories of sexual orientation—heterosexual, homosexual, bisexual—the respondents could choose "something else." Among female participants, 1.3 percent identified as homosexual and 2.8 percent identified as bisexual, while 2.3 percent of male participants identified as homosexual and 1.8 percent identified as bisexual. Interestingly, a mighty minority (3.9 percent) of participants (combined male and female) chose "something else" as their sexual orientation. A further 1.8 percent did not endorse any of the categories offered to them (i.e., heterosexual, homosexual, bisexual, or "something else"). These figures may represent an important piece of the prevalence puzzle of asexuality. However, it is also important to bear in mind that "something else" (or a nonresponse) is vague, and using "identification" is problematic if one wants a relatively conceptually clean definition of sexual orientation that would also encompass an asexual orientation (see also chapter 2).

Now let's consider a general issue that may affect the reporting rate of asexuality, regardless of how it is defined. This issue is *volunteer bias*, and it is related to an issue mentioned above: people who choose to participate in sex studies (relative to those who choose not to) are more liberal in their sex attitudes, more interested in sex, and have more sexual experience (e.g., Bogaert, 1996; Morokoff, 1986; Saunders, Fisher, Hewitt, & Clayton, 1985). This issue is called *volunteer bias* because there is bias in favor of recruiting certain types of participants over others in human research studies. Volunteer bias is a potential problem in all human studies, but it has been argued to be especially problematic in studies of sexuality, which, as mentioned previously, seem prone to over-sample sexually liberal people. If so, the rate of asexuality may be higher than reported in sexual surveys, because people with less liberal sexual attitudes/behavior often decline to participate in such surveys. This is even true in the best studies we have: national probability samples, such as

NATSAL-I and NATSAL-II. For example, the so-called refusal rate—those who were contacted to participate but chose not to—in NATSAL-I was about 30 percent; in NATSAL-II, it was even slightly higher (around 35 percent). Thus, a high number of asexual people may not have agreed to participate in past sexual surveys because they were uninterested in or uncomfortable with the subject matter of these surveys: sex. *A sex survey? Why on earth would I want to do that?* It is a bit like getting a call from the Professional Golfers Association wanting to talk about your favorite courses, your handicap, the type of clubs you use, and your preferred brand of ball, and you declining to participate because you don't play and, frankly, don't want to start playing. *What! You don't want to talk intimately about golf for an hour?* (I use this as an example because I am a golfer but have, over the years, somewhat reluctantly come to terms with the fact that the game is, evidently, not of interest to everyone.)

Interestingly, then, some of the best sexuality data, including the best data on the prevalence of asexuality, may come from national samples that are not, per se, sex surveys. Thus, the NSFG survey mentioned above may be a better survey to assess asexuality than the NATSAL surveys, because the former was a "general health survey." However, as mentioned, this study also has its problems: no clear asexuality measure and a restriction of age range.

So, how many people are asexual? We do not know for sure, as there are different problems—such as volunteer bias, lack of a long-term time frame, and questions about how best to define asexuality—with each of the national studies mentioned above. However, the original estimate (Bogaert, 2004) of 1 percent may not be a bad one, all things considered, and it is possible that it may underestimate the true number of asexual people.[3]

But why is the prevalence of sexual minorities of interest at all? Does it matter how many people are gay, lesbian, bisexual, straight, or asexual? Yes, it does—both to scientists and nonscientists alike, and for a variety of reasons. One scientific reason is that sexual orientation is a fundamental aspect of human variability, and thus understanding the prevalence of heterosexuality, bisexuality, homosexuality, and asexuality helps to map the distribution of human sexual variability. Second, the prevalence of sexual minorities is of interest to groups who want to use the figures to support a political cause or a social issue. For example, some anti-gay groups are interested in the rate of homosexuality (particularly if it is low) to try to demonstrate that homosexuality is statistically rare and thus gay people should be considered abnormal, pathological, or at least a fringe element of society.[4] In contrast, gay, lesbian, and asexuality advocacy groups are interested in the rate (particularly if it is high) to demonstrate the opposite: that being a sexual minority is not uncommon or statistically abnormal, and that sexual minorities form a significantly large segment of society. A third reason why the sexual minority prevalence rate is of interest is because of the science of demography. As mentioned in the introduction (chapter 1), demographers are interested in how many members of sexual minorities there are, because their prevalence relates to, among other things, trends in marriage and fertility (how many people marry and/or have children). Fourth, the prevalence of sexual minorities relates to physical health issues and, thus, is of interest to epidemiologists and health-care workers. A recent example concerns male homosexuality and the HIV/AIDS pandemic. HIV/AIDS in Western societies has been largely related to male-male sexual contact. As such, understanding the prevalence of male homosexuality can help with understanding the causes of this disease and tracking changes in it in Western societies. Indeed, some of the national probability surveys of human sexuality mentioned above (e.g., NATSAL-I, NHSLS) (Johnson et al., 1994; Laumann et al., 1994) were funded by government agencies wanting accurate information on people's behavior as it relates to HIV/AIDS. Fifth, prevalence rates of sexual minorities are also important from a mental health perspective. As many people are aware, discrimination against gays, lesbians, and bisexuals is still a societal problem (Herek, 2000; Herek, 2002). Moreover, the "coming out" process is often stressful for sexual minorities. For example, one study found that a very high percentage of gay men (approximately 90 percent) felt troubled, many "extremely so," when coming out to their parents (D'Augelli, 1991). But what about asexuals—are they also subject to discrimination and to significant stress in coming out? There is much less research on this issue but, interestingly, there is recent evidence that asexual people may, in fact, be viewed more negatively than gays, bisexuals, and lesbians (see more in chapter 7) (MacInnis & Hodson, in press). Thus, accurate knowledge of sexual minority prevalence rates helps workers in mental health care gauge the size of, and potentially address, this mental health concern facing society.

In the final part of this chapter, I explore people's reactions to the idea that a certain percentage (e.g., 1 percent) of humanity is, in fact, asexual, including the "As if!" reaction mentioned earlier.

At the outset, though, let me offer one qualification. Despite the "As if!" reaction introduced this chapter, I do not want to leave the reader with the impression that all people have reacted with disbelief—many, if not most, people have seemed to accept that a small minority of humanity is asexual. Also, as I will discuss later in the chapter, some have actually indicated surprise that the original figure (1 percent) is so low. Relatedly, my sense is that some people have reacted with relief to the suggestion that a certain percentage of humanity is asexual. *Why relief?* I think some people may feel relieved, if only secretly, to know that not all people are extremely sexual beings, or that one does not have to be extremely sexual to be a contented, functioning person in society. There is a lot of pressure to be very sexual in our society (e.g., from the mass media; see also chapter 7 on identity formation), so knowing that some people are completely asexual, and perhaps relatively happy being so, may be a bit of a relief for some (average) sexual people. It takes the pressure off them to know that, by comparison, their sex lives are fairly active, and that they do not have to be the super-sexed athlete the media often suggest is the norm.

But let's come back to the doubters and deconstruct the "As if!" reaction: Why do some people feel that less than 1 percent of the population is asexual, and who exactly are these doubters?

One explanation for the "As if!" reaction is that the doubters are right, and thus their skepticism of this figure may not be misplaced. After all, we may not have an accurate tally of the number of asexual people. Even the sarcasm inherent in this "As if!" reaction may not be misplaced, as the figure could be lower (perhaps even much lower) than 1 percent. Thus, these doubters could be wise people, knowledgeable in the ways of the world, and not easily taken in by potentially misguided scientific claims.

A second explanation is that this skepticism reflects, at least partly, a human tendency to believe that everyone must be just like us. Social psychologists have labeled this bias the *false consensus* effect (e.g., Ross, Greene, & House, 1977). Thus, if *I* feel sexual, then everyone else must be sexual too, or just as sexual as I am. So, it is an understandable reaction that some people can't believe in asexuality, because everyone, at times, is prone to these kinds of false consensus reactions. We all live in our little insulated worlds, and it is sometimes hard to imagine that something very different exists beyond it.[5]

But who exactly are the most likely doubters? Interestingly, they seem to be, almost invariably, men. Perhaps this says something about male sexuality: that it emerges with such a punch in the groin at adolescence, thanks largely to pubertal testosterone (Udry, Billy, Morris, Groff, & Raj, 1985), and generally sustains itself as such a major force in many men's lives, that some men cannot perceive it could be otherwise in others; hence, they have a *false consensus* that everyone has a high, male-like, sexual attraction and drive.

Conversely, more women than men have questioned whether this figure was too low. Is this also a false consensus effect? If women have a lower sex drive than men, and their sexual attractions are more flexible than men's (see chapter 6), perhaps they assume that a disproportionately high number of people are similarly inclined (i.e., have low sexual drives and/or lack sexual attraction)? *Hmmm, only this low, huh? I expected the figure to be much higher. . . .*[6]

I've also noted that some gay men seem to be the most suspicious of asexual people. This is partially understandable because gay men, of course, are also part of the high testosterone brood—men. But there may be other reasons as well. First, openly gay people, especially those with a bit of seasoning in the sexual marketplace, are often astute enough to know that people claiming one sexual identity (e.g., "I am bisexual," "I am heterosexual") at one point in their lives may "come out" as gay years later. I, too, do not discount the possibility that some asexual people, or those who identify as such, might be gay people in waiting, although I suspect that this does not apply to the majority of asexual people.

An additional reason why some gay men may be opposed to accepting a 1 percent (or more) prevalence rate may concern justice sensitivity. Gay and lesbian people have often fought hard for the right to be accepted in Western society as a visible minority. Thus, although most gays and lesbians seem very accepting of sexual variations, some may be justifiably sensitive to issues related to their own rights and recognition. Now there is a new kid on the block, perhaps encroaching on their hard-fought and hard-won space. Does yet another sexual minority in some way diminish the status of the *original* sexual minority group? Perhaps some gay and lesbians believe so, if only on an implicit level. Relatedly, I expect that all humans, as social psychologists have argued, have a tendency to dislike the "out-group" and, sadly and concomitantly, to force to the back of the metaphorical bus ever more marginalized groups, even among those who believe that they themselves are near the back of the bus already.

SUMMARY

Even when we rely on information from national probability samples, we cannot know for sure how many asexual people exist, although my original estimate of 1 percent may not be a bad figure to work with for now. There are various reasons (e.g., health, demographic, political) why such prevalence figures are important and of interest; thus, the tallying and head counting of sexual minorities is not likely to go away soon. Why people believe or do not believe (i.e., the "As if!" reaction) in the current estimates of sexual minorities may have less to do with the quality of the scientific studies surveying this issue (although this factor should not be discounted) and more to do with human cognitive biases (e.g., the false consensus effect). The fact that sexuality so often and so strongly evokes these biases—even when discussing asexuality—reaffirms a main theme in this book: sex is deeply embedded in our psyches and our cultures, and not just in our genitals.

NOTES

1. This code is subversive at least in part because it turns the heterosexual world's discrimination against gays and lesbians on its ear. It is empowering (for some) because it often "steals" back the negative words (e.g., queer) that others have used against gays and lesbians for many years, and thus reclaims for gays and lesbians the right to use their own language in their own way.

2. As we noted in chapter 3, Kinsey placed a heavy (but not sole) emphasis on behavior in defining sexual orientation, so the caveats we raised about primarily "behavioral" definitions of sexual orientations should be kept in mind. And, of course, remember that Kinsey's sample was not representative of the broader U.S. population.

3. Although they should be viewed with a high degree of caution, there have also been a number of relatively modern nonrepresentative surveys that provide some information on the prevalence of asexuality. In late 2004, when the popular press surrounding the issue of asexuality became heightened, CNN conducted an Internet poll on sexual identity. They asked people to report their sexual orientation using four categories (straight/heterosexual, gay/homosexual, bisexual, or asexual). Approximately 110,000 people responded, of whom 6 percent reported that they identify themselves as "asexual" (CNN.com, 2004, October 14). Furthermore, using a U.S.-

based convenience sample of adults, one researcher reported that about 10 percent of women and 5 percent of men indicated that they lacked sexual attraction to either men or women (Nurius, 1983).

4. It should be pointed out that interest in these figures for political purposes is partly based on faulty logic. Statistical rarity, at least by itself, is not a good criterion for demonstrating pathology or the lack of it—consider, for example, extreme musical talent (see more on this in chapter 9). It is also illogical (and insensitive) to treat a group of individuals unfairly and inhumanely based solely on their prevalence rate in society.

5. Even though we all have this bias to some degree, one of the more intriguing experiences in life is, arguably, being faced with the incontrovertible evidence of human diversity. It often makes our lives richer, although perhaps a lot less predictable. So, while we may want to believe (and hope) that everyone is like us, when faced with evidence to the contrary, it may be initially threatening but, ultimately, often life affirming.

6. In the last two paragraphs, I expect I offended both men and women. In my defense, although lots of variability exists within each sex, there is also strong evidence that men, on average, have a higher sex drive than women do, and that women are more flexible in their sex drives/attractions (see also chapter 6) (Baumeister, 2000; Baumeister, Catanese, & Vohs, 2001).

FIVE

To Masturbate or Not to Masturbate

In this chapter, I ask and perhaps answer a series of seemingly dumb questions about masturbation. I do so to try to understand masturbation as a sexual phenomenon, but also to understand some of the variability in asexuality.

My first dumb question is this: What is the *purpose* of masturbation? This first question about the rather delicate subject of masturbation is, at least on the surface, "dumb," because there is, of course, in many people's minds no real purpose to masturbation, aside from simple pleasure; it just feels good, and that's why people do it. But from an evolutionary standpoint, it is a good question, because the existence of any form of sexual variability without clear reproductive benefits (e.g., homosexuality, asexuality, *and* masturbation) puzzles scientists. After all, how could a sexual variation without potential procreative sustainability compete with one—heterosexual intercourse—that has obvious and built-in procreative sustainability (the replication of genes in the form of children) over millions of years of human evolutionary history? So, masturbation seemingly serves no obvious reproductive purpose, yet it exists. Thus, masturbation misses the (evolutionary) point. (And sometimes, in the case of men, messes the point.)

So the answer, "because it feels good," begs another question: *Why* does it feel good? Or, at least, *why* does it feel good enough to make people do it, even sometimes when there is an available partner? Before we answer this question, let's give a little background on the incidence and frequency of masturbation. In the classic survey conducted in the

55

United States by the pioneer sex researcher Alfred Kinsey, nearly all the men and about 60 percent of the women indicated that they had masturbated at least once (Kinsey, Pomeroy, & Martin, 1948; Kinsey, Pomeroy, Martin, & Gebhard, 1953). Indeed, one of the great cultural shocks of the 1950s, summarized in Kinsey's book *Sexual Behavior in the Human Female*, was that a majority of women had masturbated. Today, people are less likely to see this fact as a revelation and more, perhaps, as a titillating curiosity. A well-conducted national survey of the United States in the 1990s, the National Health and Social Life Survey, sometimes considered the modern follow-up to Kinsey's work, indicated that 75 percent of women had masturbated (Laumann, Gagnon, Michael, & Michaels, 1994). So, there is support for the notion that masturbation is a common recreation, rivaling—dare I say?—baseball (or hockey if you're from Canada) as a national pastime.

Returning to our original question, what is the purpose of masturbation? It is true that masturbation does, for most people, feel good and thus serves "the purpose" of pleasure enhancement. It is also true that other factors, including the availability of a partner, can influence masturbation frequency. So, some people do it, partly as a substitute for an unavailable partner.[1]

Beyond these perhaps rather obvious reasons, the ubiquity of the act suggests that masturbation may be evolutionarily adaptive or serve a reproductive "function," or at least not be detrimental to one's reproductive success. Indeed, there is likely a purpose to masturbation beyond mere pleasure enhancement or replacement for a lack of sexual partner. In adolescence or young adulthood (particularly if accompanied by fantasy), it may serve as a form of sexual "rehearsal," or a kind of mental acting out of sexual scenes (*First I'll kiss her like this, then I'll stroke her like that* . . .). Thus, it may create or at least reinforce important sexual scripts, potentially to be played out with partners later on in life (see also chapter 2). In other words, as an actor learns his role—what he needs to say and do—from a TV script, we learn potentially adaptive sequences of behavior, along with how to deal with behavioral contingencies (*If this happens, do this; if that happens, do that* . . .), partially through fantasies.[2]

Sometimes the fantasies are mere snippets of what, in real life, would comprise a longer sequence of behavior. So, for a heterosexual male adolescent, it may be as simple as imagining kissing a woman, stroking her inner thighs, and rubbing her vulva. These imaginings may ingrain into his psyche a short sexual script, the elements and order of which would be adaptive to act out if he were to encounter an opportunity to engage in sexual behavior with a member of the other sex.

Sometimes the imaginings are more elaborate. So, a young heterosexual man may have elaborate "harem-like" fantasies of having a bevy of beautiful young women as playthings at his sexual beck and call. If a heterosexual man ever had a chance to encounter and then enter this situation (i.e., to be a harem master), it would be, at least from an evolutionary perspective, a good idea for him to act out this script, as it would be a procreative gold mine: men's genes would be replicated at a high frequency by mating with many young women. Men have a relatively low reproductive/parental investment (e.g., lots of sperm that are easily replaced), so, from the perspective of procreation, it is in a man's interest to sow his seed among as many reproductively viable women as possible (Buss & Schmitt, 1993; Symons, 1979; Trivers, 1972). Conversely, women have a relatively high reproductive/parental investment (e.g., must gestate a fetus for nine months inside her own body), so it is usually in their best interest to be picky sexually, potentially securing a man's resources to help with raising their offspring and only mating with men of high-quality genes. Thus, it would be in an average heterosexual woman's advantage to form a sexual/romantic bond with, say, Brad Pitt if she had the opportunity in real life, given the high quality of his genes (*My gosh, is he cute!*) and his excellent resources (*My gosh, is he rich!*). So, a young woman's fantasies about Brad Pitt or similar men, even if they might irk her husband (if he knew), would be adaptive, as they help in rehearsing reproductively beneficial actions/scenes in case she ever encountered them.

In sum, it is not surprising that men and women create or are drawn to fantasies of this kind: they help to create or reinforce sexual scripts that, if they unfolded in real life, could be a huge boon, reproductively speaking.[3]

Masturbation may also have physical health benefits. Men's prostate health later in life may be related to frequency of masturbation early in life (Walsh, 2004). Thus, frequent "flushing out" of the prostate gland (an important internal reproductive organ providing some of the content of semen) in early adolescence and young adulthood may serve a man well, although there is some conflicting evidence of this benefit (Dimitropoulou et al., 2009). Masters and Johnson (1966) argued that, for women, masturbation can be a good remedy for pelvic congestion, which contributes to menstrual cramps and tension. Similarly, men may also derive some relief through masturbation from muscular tension and pelvic congestion caused by sexual arousal. This explanation for masturbation—relief from tension and congestion—partly blurs the distinction between health and pleasure, as tension reduction is potentially healthy, but it also can be pleasurable. Finally, there is some evidence that sexual activity, including masturbation, is associated with heart health (Davey, Frankel, & Yarnell, 1997).

In sum, all of these factors—pleasure, the creation and rehearsal of sexual scripts, and various health benefits—may have conspired to create an impulse in humans to be the rather compulsive masturbators that they are (call it a "psychological masturbation mechanism").

My second dumb question is this: Do asexual people masturbate? This may seem like a bit of an odd question, given that asexual people should have little interest in sex (right?). Despite the seeming peculiarity of it, the answer is, yes, some asexual people masturbate. In a recent study by Lori Brotto and her colleagues, about 80 percent of asexual men reported that they had masturbated, and about 70 percent of asexual women reported they had masturbated (Brotto, Knudson, Inskip, Rhodes, & Erskine, 2010). There was no comparison group of sexual people in their study, but these percentages (80 percent; 70 percent) were only somewhat lower than the percentage of people who reported masturbating in a national sample of the United States population. This is an extraordinarily high percentage, given that asexual people are perceived to have no sexual desire! However, although interesting, these findings may not be representative of the asexual population, as they likely represent only those who frequent the AVEN website (the most popular asexual website). These individuals may be more liberal and adventuresome (e.g., more curious about masturbation) than average asexual people. There was no information on masturbation available in my first study of asexuality using the NATSAL-I data (Bogaert, 2004) (see also chapter 4). However, in the follow-up to this representative British sample (NATSAL-II), I found that 42 percent of asexual people had masturbated in the last month (Bogaert, in press-a). This percentage is, as perhaps you might expect, lower than the percentage for sexual people (70 percent). Also, this 42 percent figure may be significantly inflated, because it reflects the responses of those asexual people who had some sexual experience with a partner; those who didn't, unfortunately, were not asked about their masturbation habits. One might expect that asexual people with no sexual experience are less likely to masturbate (thus, the 42 percent should be a lower figure), because sexual behaviors tend to correlate with one another (i.e., people with more sexual experience also tend to masturbate more). But we can't know this for sure. The broad and more important point, however, is that some percentage—perhaps a substantial percentage!—of asexual people masturbate, or at least have tried it once or twice.

One important point to take away from the research on masturbation among asexual people is that it reinforces the notion that asexuality is a diverse phenomenon: there are some who do engage in masturbation (a seemingly sexual behavior) and some who do not. In other words, there are different types of asexual people.

My next question, then, not really that dumb, is this: *Why* do some asexual people masturbate? It's not really a dumb question because asexuality should be associated, presumably, with low, if not totally absent, sexual activity, and thus pondering why some asexual people engage in this form of sexual expression is a legitimate question.

Of the main reasons for masturbation (i.e., pleasure, rehearsal, health) mentioned above, which is the most likely to explain why some asexual people masturbate? The rehearsal function is not likely to be of ultimate importance for many asexual people, because they are not inclined to play out elaborate sexual scripts with partners.[4] However, releasing physical tension and health are likely important. In line with this explanation, some asexual people discuss masturbation in a health-oriented, utilitarian fashion: for instance, they sometimes engage in it to "clean out the plumbing" (Brotto et al., 2010, p. 611). Here is a similar quote from another asexual person discussing masturbation on AVEN: "It just feels like there's a tension or something my body needs to release, but my mind has no interest in it whatsoever" (AnyOtherName, 2010, August 22).

This explanation for masturbation—as a pure physical release—may seem a bit clinical and devoid of other elements typically comprising a sexual experience. Yet it is important to keep in mind some of the distinctions made in chapter 2—namely, that one can have physical arousal (e.g., gain an erection, have lubrication, an orgasm) without necessarily having, for example, sexual attraction to (or desire for) others.

Such quotes also suggest that the sensation of masturbation experienced by some asexual people may not be particularly "pleasurable," at least in not in an intensely "sexual" way. It may still feel good, to some degree, in the same way that releasing any tension and buildup feels good to people (i.e., as a relief). And, as mentioned, some sexual people may masturbate, at times, for this reason: merely to release tension and pelvic congestion, and less for the intense sexual pleasure of it.

For other asexual people, there may still be sexual feelings and/or intense physical pleasure, similar to how most sexual people feel when masturbating or having sex with a partner. Thus, another reason why asexual people masturbate is relatively straightforward and similar to why sexual people do it: for physical pleasure. At this point, however, we do not have good data on what percentage of asexual people derive intense (sexual) pleasure from masturbation. I expect that some asexual people do, and if so, this would again suggest that asexuality is a diverse phenomenon: some asexual people do not masturbate, some masturbate with "sexual" pleasure, and some masturbate without much sexual pleasure. If it is true that some asexual people do still experience intense (sexual) pleasure, it is again important to keep in mind some of the basic distinctions raised earlier: that one can have a deeply (subjective) sexually pleasurable feeling of arousal without necessarily having a deep sexual connection with or attraction to partners (in other words, one can have that sexual feeling of arousal and still be "asexual" as I define it; see chapter 2). Relatedly, it is certainly true that sexual people sometimes have sex and masturbate without necessarily connecting the sexual pleasure to anyone specifically. So, for example, sexual men and women may enjoy the sheer physical sensation of intercourse without necessarily being attracted to their partners. A very sexually experienced gay man once recounted to me that he enjoyed vaginal intercourse with women more than anal intercourse with men, because of the sheer physical sensation of his penis being stimulated by the tubular architecture of the vagina, along with the lubrication it provides when a woman is physically aroused. Thus, as we have suggested, subjective physical pleasure and sensation associated with arousal can be divorced from one's attraction to others.

My next dumb question is one that I actually posed to an asexual man: What do asexual people masturbate *to*? This was clearly a bit of an odd question for him. For most masturbators (well, okay, much of the planet), this question is relatively easy to answer. They often masturbate to a fantasy, a conjured-up image of a favorite person (or group of people), a picture, moving or otherwise, of sexual scenes. In other words, they masturbate to some sort of image or story of what they are sexually attracted to. For example, a young woman may masturbate to a story line of an erotic novel she has read, perhaps replacing the heroine with herself in the fantasy, or, as mentioned, to an image of hunky Brad Pitt. A young man may masturbate to the image of a seductively posed nude woman in a magazine or on the Internet, or, as mentioned above, to harem-like fantasies.

This is evidently not so for many asexual people who masturbate. In fact, the asexual person, perplexed, did not answer at first, and then only responded when I saw him on the next occasion, after having thought about it, and discussing it with some asexual people on the AVEN website. He suggested that many asexual people just masturbate *to* nothing in particular. This makes sense, as asexual people with sexual desire (or urges, but lacking sexual attraction) do not direct this desire toward anyone (or anything). So, the question of what an asexual person masturbates *to* is, perhaps understandably, nonsensical, or best answered with "nothing in particular" (or at least nothing of particular sexual relevance to the asexual person).

This *nondirected* masturbation also reinforces the idea that some, perhaps many, asexual people often do not have sexual fantasies, or at least not in the same way that sexual people usually have them. There is some research by Lori Brotto and her colleagues suggesting that some asexual people do have fantasies (Brotto et al., 2010), but it is unclear from this research whether the fantasies co-occur with masturbation, whether they are primarily "romantic," and what function they serve (see also discussion below). Interestingly, this nondirected masturbation also reinforces the idea that masturbation in asexual people probably does not serve a "rehearsal" function that prepares them to act upon scenarios that they might encounter in real life. And why would it, given that asexual people do not need to sexually "practice" sequences of behaviors with preferred partners?

Here is a follow-up, not-so-dumb, question: What if some (i.e., a small percentage) asexual people have fantasy-based masturbation? What would this mean? In addition to understanding sexual fantasies as important for the development and rehearsal of sexual scripts, human sexuality researchers are interested in sexual fantasies because we know that their content says something about what people are truly attracted to. Sexual fantasies are more important than actual behavior—what we actually do with a partner—in this regard, because partnered behavior represents a compromise of the individuals engaged in that behavior. Fantasies often do not represent any compromise: they usually only spring from the individual's own desires and attractions; thus, they are a (relatively) pure reflection of one's true attractions.

Pornography contains commercially produced sexual fantasies, or at least fantasy-enhancement material. This is especially true for men. If so, the type of pornography men view and/or masturbate to should be an indicator of their attractions. Gay men are attracted to men, so, not surprisingly, they will view images of naked men or men engaged in sex. Similarly, heterosexual men are attracted to women, so they will view images of naked women, men having sex with women, or two or more women having sex together. This attraction/porn relationship can be used as a diagnostic tool of a person's sexual orientation. If, for example, an adolescent male professes to be heterosexual and yet is found with a large stash of gay porn, the content of his stash trumps (or at least calls into question) his professed heterosexual attractions, at least as far as many sexual orientation researchers are concerned. Interestingly, this diagnostic tool can also be used to diagnose deviant sexual attractions. If a man professes to be attracted to adults but has a stash of child pornography (and little or no adult-oriented pornography), then the content of this stash can be used to help determine that the man is likely a pedophile (Seto, Cantor, & Blanchard, 2006).[5]

The pornography/attraction relationship is more complicated for women, especially given that they are often less visually oriented in their sexual response than men (see more on sex/gender differences in chapter 6). But the overall point about sexual fantasies as a window into the sexual attraction "soul" still holds up reasonably well. If so, persistent sexual fantasies in asexual people, and particularly in asexual men, may be a partial way of determining whether they have some level of attraction for men or women, or some unusual thing, such as an object or an event (see chapter 12).

Interestingly, the fact that the asexual person I referred to above actually did not comprehend my question about "what do you masturbate *to*" indicates to me that he does indeed lack sexual fantasy (and sexual scripts). Thus, he is *asexual* as I define it (i.e., a lack of sexual attraction), and even though he may masturbate, he does not direct his masturbation to something or someone. Also, that other asexual people like him do not seem to fantasize in any systematic or directed way, or don't masturbate altogether, indicates that many asexual people do not have sexual attractions, typical or atypical in nature.

However, my discussions with people who identify as asexual (along with some of the discussion on AVEN) suggest that some do have consistent fantasies or choose specific stimuli (e.g., pornography) to which they masturbate repeatedly. Also, as mentioned above, some level of fantasy does occur in asexual people (Brotto et al., 2010). This fact raises questions about their sexual attractions and whether some of these individuals might have unusual sexual attractions, called *paraphilias* (see also chapter 10).

Interestingly, when the fantasies do occur in asexual people in a consistent or systematic way, they are often, although not always, still of a "disconnected" sort. That is, these people often view themselves as not being part of the sexual acts they are fantasizing about or viewing (e.g., pornography). In other words, they *themselves* are not connected to anything or anyone sexual. It is as if their own identities—who they are as individuals—are not sexual (*they* are not attracted to anyone or anything), but their bodies, or (more correctly) aspects of their mind related to sexual arousal but not fully connected to their identity, may still need sexual stimulation for them to masturbate (and perhaps receive pleasure). This "disconnect" of identity from masturbation and sexual fantasy is very intriguing. To me, it still suggests that these people lack sexual attraction on some level (and thus have an "asexual" orientation), because their identity—who they are as individuals—is not sexually connected to anyone or anything. However, we will take up these fascinating questions and their implications—such as whether these people have a paraphilia and whether they can still truly be labeled asexual (i.e., lacking in sexual attraction)—further in chapter 10 (Bogaert, 2008).

SUMMARY

There are probably a number of different functions (e.g., pleasure, script development and rehearsal, health benefits) to human masturbation, this most common of sexual behaviors. Although they do not masturbate to the same degree as sexual people do (as one might expect), asexual people may have a masturbation history, and some may masturbate at a relatively high frequency. This fact reinforces the idea that what might be termed "sexual" behaviors, such as masturbation, are not necessarily completely absent in asexual people. It also lends support to the idea that what is termed a "sexual" behavior may, sometimes, be devoid of intense sexual feelings (even in sexual people), and yet it may still serve a function (such as health or physical release). The fact that some asexual people masturbate and some asexual people do not also reinforces the idea that asexuality is a diverse phenomenon. In other words, there are different types of asexual people, some of whom have desire (or at least impulses and urges, even if they are not intensely "sexual" desires) and some who do not. There may be a core element to all asexual people, however: a lack of sexual attraction (see also chapter 2). Finally, the ideas brought forward in this chapter confirm the notion that researchers should be aware that some people who identify as asexual may have a paraphilia, a sexual attraction to something unusual. One way of finding out more about whether some masturbating asexual people have paraphilias is to study their fantasies, which reveal (often secret) attractions. More research is also needed to verify some of the conclusions I have drawn in this chapter, in part because the data on which I have based these conclusions are incomplete and/or somewhat informal in nature (e.g., quotes from relatively few individuals). So more questions, even seemingly dumb ones, need to be asked.

NOTES

1. However, note that a lack of a partner is not a good proxy for high frequency of masturbation, as sexual behaviors tend to correlate with one another, so those who have frequent sex with a partner also, on average, masturbate more. But the main point here is that masturbation can, at least for some, serve as a substitute for an unavailable partner.

2. Masturbation, then, is like all "play" activity in that it is more frequent in younger versus older people, but the seeming insignificance of the act belies the fact that it partially prepares one for later, adult-oriented challenges. Thus, it is not surprising that our fantasies often match or closely resemble what might be best for us from an evolutionary perspective, even if this fantasy world never exists in real life.

3. Even though our fantasies often resemble what might be "best" for us, at least from an evolutionary perspective, modern society also has the capacity to make our fantasies maladaptive. The modern media, with their high-tech sophistication and super-realistic images, may make our fantasies more real and powerful than our

brains could ever conjure. Thus, along with ingraining sexual scripts, modern media probably raise our expectations and, at times, make us too unrealistic about what to expect in real-life sexual encounters. Thus, these fantasies may be somewhat maladaptive in modern society, even if they would have been adaptive in in our evolutionary past. After all, realistically, we can't all mate with Brad Pitt!

4. This is not to imply that when (sexual) adolescents engage in masturbation with fantasies, they do so with the conscious intent of building sexual scripts into their psyches. Rather, this is done unconsciously; it just happens, especially after the fantasy/script is paired with (often repeatedly!) rewarding sexual pleasure and orgasm. If unconscious, one could argue that asexual people still retain the ancient mechanisms of masturbation (even an incentive to masturbate), which would have served this rehearsal function in our evolutionary past, but which is a somewhat useless byproduct for them now. However, as we will see later in this chapter, asexual people may be less likely to build sexual scripts into their psyches, because (perhaps not surprisingly) their masturbation is often without fantasy.

5. People often make a "causal inference" between a person's exposure to pornography and his or her sexual attractions. So people may assume that exposure to pornography causes attraction to this material. For example, it is often assumed that an adolescent boy or a young man's exposure to child pornography causes a sexual interest in children. Theoretically, this is possible, but most sex researchers are cautious about making such causal inferences, as they know that when two events co-occur—a correlation—this is not evidence of causation. When a correlation of this kind occurs, especially repeatedly (e.g., a man with a large stash of child porn collected over many different years), this may merely be good evidence that an attraction to this material occurs, and that we need to be alerted to that fact.

SIX

Sex and Gender

The holy grail of sexual mysteries is female sexuality. Sex researchers regularly salivate, like Pavlov's dogs, at the prospect of solving this mystery of mysteries. Even Sigmund Freud, who was never one to shy away from asserting his knowledge of human behavior, recognized his ignorance and famously queried, "What do they want?"

Some modern examples: There's a relatively famous song by a female singer—"I know what boys like; I know what guys want" (The Waitresses, n.d.). There is no equivalent song about female desire sung by a male singer. There is a well-known picture (e.g., on the Internet) of two black boxes, one of which has a sole "on/off" switch and is labeled "the man"; the other has a vast array of dials and knobs and is labeled "the woman." I show this picture in my human sexuality class when I address differences in sexuality between men and women. Aside from a few students with blank looks, they laugh. The humor occurs because they know, on some level, that inside the woman's black box (aptly named) is that mystery of mysteries—the complex nature of women's desire—and that inside the man's black box (not so aptly named) is, well, one thick wire leading to that on/off switch.

In this chapter, I discuss the mysterious nature of women's (and men's!) sexuality, particularly as it is relates to asexuality. In other words, I explore how sex and gender affect sexuality and asexuality.

Let's start with some context and definitions. Sex and its cultural cousin, gender, are complex constructs. *Sex* usually refers to the biological differences between males and females: penis and vagina; XY (male) and

XX (female) chromosomes; male hormones (e.g., testosterone) and female hormones (e.g., estrogens); and so forth. So, *sex* refers to male and female anatomy and their biological processes. *Gender* usually pertains to the expectations that a culture places on males and females to behave in a specific way; in other words, what are the typical *masculine* and *feminine* roles in society? *Gender* also often relates to one's psychological feelings or states as a male or a female. So, for example, people who perceive themselves as a man have a male *gender identity*.

You may be thinking, *This is easy enough, so why are they such complex concepts?* Well, let's deconstruct these concepts a bit. First, are there just *two* sexes? Another one of my dumb questions, you ask? (For more dumb questions, see chapter 5 on masturbation.) Well, actually, despite what most people believe, some experts suggest that two sexes are too limiting and that perhaps as many as five different sexes exist in human beings. Anne Fausto-Sterling, a biologist at Brown University, advocated this position, albeit one that she later admitted was argued tongue-in-cheek and to prove a broader point (1993; 2000). That broader point was that the rigid binary system of two sexes is not complex enough to understand the variation that exists in biological sex. John Money, the famous psychologist and sexologist, also pointed out the ambiguity in biological sex by noting that whether we call someone a male or female can depend on a variety of biological variables, not all of which are necessarily aligned or consistent (Money, Hampson, & Hampson, 1957). So, one can define sex by XY (male) or XX (female) chromosomes, but what if the gonads—testes or ovaries—do not match up with a standard XY or XX chromosomal profile in a given person? In other words, what if someone has XY chromosomes but also has ovaries? What if someone has the internal reproductive organs normally reserved for women (e.g., fallopian tubes and uterus) but has external male genitalia? This kind of sexual ambiguity, sometimes called *intersexuality*, is surprisingly prevalent (i.e., about 1–2 percent of births) (Fausto-Sterling, 2000), and it illustrates the need, when speaking about biological sex, for language and concepts capable of handling complexity.

There is also ambiguity when we refer to male and female hormones. The so-called female hormones, the estrogens that are produced by the ovaries in women (e.g., estradiol), also exist in men; in fact, testosterone, a so-called male hormone, is converted to estradiol in men under the influence of the enzyme aromatase. Women also produce testosterone, so this hormone is also not fully sex specific—that is, it is not limited to men.

There is another level of ambiguity, or at least complexity, associated with both sex and gender. Some people are born with all of their biological variables consistent with traditional maleness or femaleness (XX, ovaries, uterus, vagina, or XY, testicles, prostate, penis), but have an internal sense of themselves or their gender identity that is inconsistent with their biological sex. These individuals are often so dissatisfied with their biological sex that they may want to alter it so that it will be consistent with their internal sense of themselves as male or female. Traditionally, these individuals have been referred to as *transsexual* in order to describe the change in biological sex that many of these individuals wanted and often accomplished through medical intervention (i.e., sex re-assignment surgery) to make their bodies, particularly their genitalia, consistent with their internal sense of themselves (Benjamin, 1966). More recently, a related word, *transgender*, has emerged. Originally, this word was used to describe people who were dissatisfied with their biological sex but who did not want to alter aspects of their bodies (e.g., via sex re-assignment surgery) (Kotula, 2002). The meaning of the term *transgender* has recently expanded, and is now a kind of "umbrella" term. This term often describes both traditional transsexuals (i.e., those who want to change biological sex and perhaps have done so) and anyone who violates traditional "gender" boundaries but does not necessarily want to alter aspects of their biological sex. Put another way, *transgender* can refer to those whose identity does not conform to their biological sex or those whose identity does not match their "gender" assigned at birth (Ekins & King, 2004). So, aside from transsexual people, the transgendered category may include those who cross-dress (e.g., drag queens or transvestites) and those who identify as, for example, "bi-gendered" or "non-gendered." It may also include the intersexual people mentioned above. Notably, there is often a "political" dimension to the term *transgender*, or a transgendered identity (Feinberg, 1992). As we describe in chapter 7, (public) identities frequently emerge out of and serve political ends.

Here is yet another ambiguity. If we find, on average, a behavioral difference between men and women, is it a *gender* difference or a *sex* difference? Well, given that this difference has to do with behavior, and presumably changes across cultures, it should be referred to as a gender difference, correct? But what if we find that this difference is influenced not just by culture but also by sex hormones—for example, high levels of testosterone in men may partially underlie their greater sex drive (Baumeister, Catanese, & Vohs, 2001). Should we then call it a *sex* difference, because it is largely (or at least partially) biologically based? The answer is obviously complex, and you may notice that researchers, for this reason, often use the phrase *sex differences* and *gender differences* seemingly inconsistently and interchangeably.

In summary, the constructs of sex and gender are quite complex, so keep this in mind as you read this chapter and ponder the differences between men and women, and consider how it all relates to asexuality. Also note that for the sake of simplicity, I use the phrase *gender differences* to refer to any behavioral differences that exist between men and women.

Not all men are alike and not all women are alike—indeed, there is a lot of variability within each—and so using people's biological sex as the only piece of information to predict their sexuality can be misleading and cause numerous errors. Yet, as the black box pictures mentioned above suggest, there are fascinating gender differences in sexuality.

One of the main differences is that men have, on average, a higher sex drive than women (Baumeister et al., 2001). In other words, men are more "sexualized" than women. Examples include the fact that men masturbate and fantasize more than women do. In one national British survey, 73 percent of men and 37 percent of women reported masturbating in the previous month (Gerressu, Mercer, Graham, Wellings, & Johnson, 2008). Relatedly, there is evidence that men (particularly young men) think about sex on a more frequent basis than women. According to one national study of the United States, more than half of men (i.e., 54 percent) think about sex several times during the day, whereas about 20 percent of women do so at about the same frequency (Laumann, Gagnon, Michael, & Michaels, 1994).

Another difference is that women's sexuality is more fluid or flexible, being more responsive to a variety of cultural and psychological factors, than men's (Baumeister, 2000). One example is that women may have a period of several months of intense sexual activity (masturbation, intercourse) and then several months of no sexual activity. This pattern is less common in men, who maintain a more constant level of sexual activity (e.g., through masturbation, one-night stands) despite, say, the ending of a romantic/sexual relationship. As psychologist Roy Baumeister notes, Kinsey himself made this observation: "Discontinuities in total [sexual] outlet are practically unknown in the histories of males" (Baumeister, 2000, pp. 681–82; Kinsey, Pomeroy, Martin, & Gebhard, 1953).

Gender differences in asexuality often seem to mirror gender differences in sexuality. In other words, the gender differences mentioned above also occur in some way between asexual men and asexual women. First, if a main gender difference is that women are less sexualized (i.e., they have lower sex drive and less sexual attraction) than men, one would expect women to be overrepresented on the extremely low end of the sexuality distribution—that is, one would expect to find more asexuality among women.

Is there evidence that women are more likely to be asexual than men? Yes, there is (Bogaert, 2004; Bogaert, in press-a; Brotto, Knudson, Inskip, Rhodes, & Erskine, 2010). For example, in my first study of asexuality, about 70 percent of the asexual people in NATSAL-I, a British national sample, were women (Bogaert, 2004). Interestingly, some indirect evidence that women are more likely than men to be asexual is that "asexual" partnerships (i.e., "Boston marriages") have been identified as a relatively common pattern among women forming relationships with women (Rothblum & Brehony, 1993), but, to my knowledge, such partnerships have never been identified as a relatively common pattern among men forming relationships with men.

What is it from a psychological or developmental perspective that makes women less likely than men to form strong sexual attractions to others? One possibility relates to masturbation differences between men and women. As suggested in chapter 5, masturbation, particularly linked with fantasy, may afford "learning/conditioning" experiences leading to more permanent sexual attractions. For example, if partners of a specific gender routinely show up in the fantasies (or pornography) to which one masturbates, then those partners may become part of one's permanent sexual attractions. If so, women who do not masturbate, or do so rarely, may not develop strong sexual attractions to others.

A biological explanation compatible with the masturbation explanation is hormones. Lower testosterone in women relative to men may create in women a less intense urge to masturbate, leading to fewer conditioning experiences and, ultimately, to fewer permanent sexual attractions to others.[1]

Another explanation relates to the flexibility in women's sexuality (Baumeister, 2000). Women's relatively flexible sexuality may make them, compared to men, more affected by social and cultural influences. Thus, if social or cultural influences are extreme, or at least atypical, women's sexuality may vary from the norm, including in the development of asexuality. Underscoring this point is the fact that women can adopt celibate lifestyles, sometimes construed as a behavioral "asexuality," for political purposes—for instance, as a protest against male-dominated society (Fahs, 2010).

Our conception of sexual orientation, or at least how it is traditionally measured, also may be relevant to gender differences in asexuality (Bogaert, 2004; Bogaert, 2006b; Bogaert, in press-a). Most sexual orientation measures imply that one's orientation is always "targeted" toward others, either males or females (or both, if bisexual). For example, a sexual orientation question may be posed as follows: "Who are you sexually attracted to?" The phrase "attracted *to*" implies an object or a "target" for our sexual interests. Thus, in this target-oriented view, usually members of one group (e.g., females) are the objects of desire, drawing our attention and fancies, and impelling us to approach members of this group for sexual activity. Yet this view of sexual orientation is, arguably, based on a male model of sexuality and thus may not capture many women's subjective experience of sexuality. This view may also affect how some women report being sexually attracted (or not being sexually attracted) to others.

At least three lines of theory and research support this target-oriented view of sexual orientation. First, there is evidence that *proceptive* desire— the urge to seek out and initiate sexual activity—may be more common in men than in women, whereas *receptive* desire—the capacity to become aroused upon encountering certain sexual circumstances—may characterize women's sexuality more so than that of men (Baumeister, 2000; Diamond, 2003b). Proceptive desire relative to receptive desire may be more conducive to a target-oriented view of sexual arousal and thus may capture the traditional (and hence more male-oriented) conceptions of sexual attraction.

Second, Meredith Chivers's recent work on men and women's arousal patterns (e.g., genital responses to erotic pictures or films) suggests that men are more target oriented in their sexuality. Her research has found that men's sexual arousal is usually directed toward one sex or another: women if they are heterosexual, men if they are gay. Women's sexual arousal is much more diffuse, and not specific to a category of sex/gender. Overall, women will respond genitally somewhat less than men to various types of erotic imagery, and usually to *both* men and women actors in the stimuli, even when the women report being exclusively heterosexual or lesbian. In other words, men's sexuality seems to have a specific category of gender as its target—a *bull's eye* in their sights. This is less so for women's sexuality—or at least women have multiple targets or bull's eyes in their sights (Chivers, Rieger, Latty, & Bailey, 2004; Chivers, Seto, & Blanchard, 2007).

Related to Meredith Chivers's work is a third line of research supporting this target-oriented view of sexual orientation: Julia Heiman's research, which shows that women are sometimes not aware of their genital responses (Heiman, 1977). Thus women may not know how their bodies are responding sexually, at least not to the same degree as men do. As a consequence, women may not associate sexual responses to a specific target (e.g., men) because they may not be aware that genital responses to a target are in fact occurring. This difference in genital response may be partially related to the way men and women's bodies work: erections are obvious, whereas vaginal responses are often more subtle.

If women's sexuality is less proceptive in nature, if their physical arousal is non-category-specific (i.e., no bull's eye in the target), and, finally, if they are not as aware of their genital responses as men are, then when women are asked to respond to questions such "who are you sexually attracted to?," perhaps it is not surprising that some women simply do not respond in a traditional (male-oriented) way: as being sexually attracted *to* either males or females (or even *to* both). Indeed, some may report or label themselves as having no sexual attraction to others (i.e., being asexual).

Let's return to some issues related to women's non-category-specific arousal. A basic question that emerges from this work is this: Why do women have such non-category-specific arousal, whereas men do not? One explanation that Chivers and colleagues favor is as follows: Nature may have designed the vagina, along with related arousal mechanisms, to prepare a woman for any kind of sexual activity that may occur, willing or otherwise. At times throughout human evolutionary history, women have been subjected to coerced sexual relations. Thus, to prevent injury, the adaptive response of the vagina, along with the brain and body mechanisms that support it, may have been to respond with expansion and lubrication at the suggestion of almost any sexual activity. Thus, the vagina is a pliably indiscriminate organ primed for any sexual contact that may arise. Indeed, Chivers and her colleagues have shown that women, unlike men, also respond genitally to chimpanzee sexual activity (Chivers, 2010). Talk about non-category-specific arousal!

If non-category-specific responding in women is an injury-preventing mechanism, then one should expect that asexual women also have such mechanisms in place, and thus also have non-category-specific responding to sexual stimuli. However, shouldn't asexual women have very different arousal patterns than sexual women? After all, if asexual women are truly "asexual," then shouldn't they have, presumably, low or absent arousal? Not necessarily. Recall that asexuality, by my and others' definitions, is a lack of sexual attraction, not a lack of physical arousal. Thus, although arousal and sexual attraction are often related, and arousal may give us information (e.g., feedback) about our sexual attractions, arousal and attraction are not the same thing. Indeed, it is clear that they are often "decoupled," and even sexual women often do not use physical arousal as a gauge of their sexual attraction/orientation—and cannot, if they are not aware of this arousal.

Lori Brotto and Morag Yule recently examined arousal patterns in asexual women. They showed that asexual women, like sexual women, indeed show non-category-specific responding to sexual stimuli—that is, some level of genital arousal to both male- and female-oriented sexual stimuli—very similar to heterosexual women and lesbians. Although this is a small study (e.g., there was no sample of asexual men), it is also an intriguing one, as the authors argue that their results give support to the notion that asexuals do not have a "disorder" as currently defined. For example, asexual women do not show low arousal (i.e., abnormally low vaginal responses) to sexual activity, as some women with sexual dysfunction do (see also chapter 11). Relatedly, the authors argue that their study provides some evidence that asexuality should be understood as a true sexual orientation, because asexual women respond in similar ways as sexual orientation groups—in other words, (nondysfunctional) lesbians and heterosexual women. Finally, this study supports the notion that non-category-specific responding (at least in terms of physical arousal) is common among women, including asexual women, and may serve a common, ancient function: to prevent injury (Brotto & Yule, 2011).

Now let's address one of the most enduring (and endearing?) gender differences in sexuality—masturbation—and examine patterns of this behavior in asexual men and women. As mentioned in chapter 5, many asexual men and women masturbate, although they do so less frequently than sexual people (e.g., Bogaert, in press-a). But most pertinent to the present chapter, asexual men report a higher frequency of masturbation than asexual women. For example, about 50 percent of asexual men report masturbating two or more times per week, versus 7 percent of asexual women (Brotto et al., 2010).

Masturbation, then, is clearly a popular pastime for both sexual and asexual men. Thus patterns of asexuality play themselves out differently in men and women, and these patterns often mirror differences between sexual men and women. The reasons why sexual men and women differ in masturbation may also explain the differences between asexual men and women in this behavior. For example, if men and women differ in sex drive (e.g., strength and/or frequency of sexual urges), then asexual men, even if they do not direct those urges toward others, may be impelled to masturbate more frequently than asexual women. Also, the inherent differences in the way men and women's bodies work—erections are obvious, whereas vaginal responses are more subtle—may be relevant. Thus, if asexual men, relative to asexual women, receive more obvious feedback that they are sexually aroused (e.g., notice their erections), they may be more likely to act on it (by masturbating), despite their lack of attraction to others.

As mentioned in chapter 5, masturbation, particularly with fantasies of recurring themes, is of interest to sexologists in part because it can reveal clues about sexual attraction. Thus masturbation among asexuals raises questions about whether some do indeed have sexual attraction to others or perhaps to something unusual (i.e., paraphilia). Given that asexual men masturbate more than asexual women, it also raises questions about whether asexual men have a potentially higher rate of paraphilias than do asexual women (also see chapter 10). If so, this pattern would also be consistent with differences between sexual men and women, as sexual men are much more likely than sexual women to have paraphilias (Cantor, Blanchard, & Barbaree, 2009).

Let's now turn to gender roles. There is evidence that gays and lesbians often do not conform to traditional gender roles, with lesbians adopting less feminine behavior patterns and gay men less masculine behavior patterns than their heterosexual counterparts (Rieger, Linsenmeier, Gygax, & Bailey, 2008). Thus, some sexual minorities do not necessarily conform to traditional gender roles, but what about asexual peo-

ple? At this point, we do not know whether asexual men are less masculine than heterosexual men, or whether asexual women are less feminine
than heterosexual women. There are standard techniques to assess
whether someone conforms to traditional gender roles—for example, if a
boy or man is interested in sports, is drawn to traditionally masculine
occupations, is more aggressive, and so on—but such techniques have
never been applied to a group of asexuals.

My hunch is that asexual people are less conforming to traditional
gender roles, on average, than heterosexual people. One of the reasons is
because traditional sexual development often may make females more
feminine and males more masculine. For example, asexual women may
be less feminine in attire, manner, and language because they lack what
Lori Brotto and I call *object-of-desire self-consciousness* (Bogaert & Brotto, in
progress). We argue that heterosexual women's sexuality is often strongly linked to perceiving themselves as an object of desire in another's eyes.
We also believe that women have a high likelihood to develop sexual
scripts—learned sequences of sexual behavior (see also chapter 5 on masturbation)—with object-of-desire themes. Indeed, my students and I
found evidence for this in a study examining heterosexual women and
men's sexual fantasies with, for example, women being more likely than
men to be turned on by having others see them as attractive, rather than
seeing someone else (i.e., their partner) as attractive. Even women's language reflects these themes, as one might expect if sexual scripts per-
meate our cognitions; after all, language and cognition (i.e., our thoughts)
are intimately linked (Bogaert, Visser, Pozzebon, & Wanless, 2011).

But what does this research on women and object-of-desire self-consciousness have to do with asexuality, and with asexual women in particular? To be sexual (and romantic) for women often emerges out of their
sense of themselves as objects of desire. So, if asexual women are not
interested in being objects of desire (and have not had socializing forces
acting on them in the same way, because of a lack of interest in sex), then
all those elements of femininity typically linked to sexuality in sexual
women will be different in asexual women. I expect, using language as an
example, that words and phrases describing beauty, attractiveness, and
body image, particularly regarding areas normally related to sexuality
(such as their curves, hair, breasts, and vulva), would be different in
asexual versus sexual women. But more than language, I expect that
asexual women's manner and attire would be different from that of aver-

age sexual women. For example, relative to sexual women, asexual women may dress in a less sexualized manner (e.g., not showing cleavage). This expected difference between sexual and asexual women in manner, attire, and language partly reflects the idea that gender (i.e., femininity) is often driven by sex and sexuality.

Related to gender roles is gender identity, the very basic sense of oneself as male or female. Of course, most people take their gender identity for granted, breezily checking off either "male" or "female" on surveys that ask about one's gender. However, as mentioned above, this is not so for a small group of people. Transgendered and intersex people, for example, often believe that their sexual anatomy is inconsistent with their gender identity; a simple "male" or "female" label may thus be inadequate.

But what about asexual people? Interestingly, although the majority of asexual people seem to identify as male or female, there is evidence that a surprisingly high percentage do not want to categorize themselves in this way. In fact, Brotto and colleagues found that approximately 13 percent did not want to identify as male or female (Brotto et al., 2010). This may not seem like an overly large percentage, but consider what proportion of the general population would not want to identify as either male or female: a small percentage (i.e., 1–2 percent or less) (Veale, 2008; Fausto-Sterling, 2000). Thus, a nontraditional gender identity is likely significantly related to asexuality. At this point, however, we do not know whether transgendered or intersex individuals make up a large proportion of asexual people.

Does the fact that gender roles and identities relate to asexuality give clues to its origin? It may. First, let's consider the potential role of biological factors—in particular, the systems involved with sexual differentiation. Sexual differentiation is the biological process whereby males become males and females become females. It occurs primarily prenatally (before birth) and then secondarily at puberty.

In sexual differentiation, some components are involved with producing female features (feminization) and male features (masculinization), but there are also processes that prevent or remove female features (defeminization) in male fetuses and prevent or remove male features (demasculinization) in female fetuses.

The exposure to hormones prenatally (in the womb) contributes to male and female sexual differentiation of both the body and brain. In other words, prenatal hormones (e.g., testosterone) will help to create male internal and external genitalia in male fetuses, while an absence of these hormones will help to create female internal and external genitalia. There is a critical time during gestation when this occurs, when fetal body tissues are sensitive to the levels of these hormones. Prenatal testosterone also affects the brain and potentially helps to create a gender role/ identity and a sexual orientation. There is also a critical time during gestation when this occurs, when fetal brain tissues are sensitive to the level of these hormones. Thus, male (XY) or female (XX) fetuses exposed to atypical levels of this hormone during critical time periods of prenatal development can have altered differentiation of the body (e.g., intersex characteristics). Similarly, atypical levels of these hormones during critical time periods may also alter brain development, thus leading to atypical gender identity (e.g., transgendered) and sexual attractions (e.g., being gay or lesbian). If so, one might also speculate that male (XY) or female (XX) fetuses exposed to atypical levels of prenatal hormones, again at critical time periods, may develop an atypical gender identity (not feeling "male" or "female"), in addition to a lack of sexual attraction (i.e., asexuality).

The traditional scientific wisdom was that female sexual differentiation, including brain differentiation, would occur if these male hormones (e.g., testosterone) were absent. Indeed, females were once seen as the "default" sex, with typical female development occurring as long as male hormones were absent. Recent evidence suggests that sexual differentiation is more complex. Male and female sexual differentiation, including brain differentiation, is indeed related to the presence or absence of male hormones, but it is also related to other prenatal mechanisms (Arnold, 2004; Kopsida, Stergiakouli, Lynn, Wilkinson, & Davies, 2009). For example, there are specific genes on the Y and X chromosomes that affect male or female brain development directly (without, for instance, affecting male hormone levels). Thus, without these additional gene-based mechanisms, male and female sexual development, including brain differentiation, would not occur in a typical fashion. If so, male (XY) or female (XX) fetuses having one or more of these genes inactivated may have altered differentiation of the body (e.g., intersex). Similarly, if it is a gene very specific to the brain, any variation or mutation of this gene may alter neural development, leading to atypical gender identity (such as being transgendered) and atypical sexual attractions, including being gay, lesbian, or asexual.

One related possibility is that altered X- or Y-linked genes or prenatal hormones, or their combination, create a form of *genderlessness* in some asexuals. In other words, some asexuals may lack sexual attraction to both males and females—a genderless sexual orientation—and lack a male or female gender identity—a genderless identity—because these biological processes have a unique effect on brain development. For example, asexuality in women may occur because of an absence/alteration of male hormones (de-masculinization) in combination with an inactivation of one or more (X) female-specific genes affecting the brain (de-feminization). Thus, some asexual women may have brains that are neither "masculine" nor "feminine." In contrast, the sexual orientations and identities of gays and lesbians may be the result of some "reversal" of a typical masculinization or feminization process. For example, prenatal exposure to a higher-than-typical level of male hormones has been argued to masculinize lesbians, including their sexual/romantic attractions (Ellis & Ames, 1987; Grimbos, Dawood, Burriss, Zucker, & Puts, 2010).

Let's also consider how environmental factors could contribute to asexuality, particularly through its association with gender identities and gender roles. One way is through asexual people's identification or dis-identification with one or both sexes. Researchers have argued that identification processes are important in sexual orientation development. Psychologist Darryl Bem asserts that if one's gender identity and gender role are traditional—for example, a boy identifying with other boys and engaging in traditional "masculine" behaviors, and so forth—it makes the opposite sex different and "exotic" and, ultimately, sexually arousing. Conversely, if a boy does not identify with boys but with girls, and engages in traditional feminine behaviors, it may make the same sex seem different and exotic and sexually arousing. Bem suggests that these processes can explain traditional sexual orientation development—in other words, how masculine boys become attracted to feminine girls. He also suggests that the same processes can explain how same-sex attraction occurs in gender nonconforming children—that is, how feminine boys become attracted to other, more masculine boys (Bem, 1996).

But what if a child has little identification with either sex? Would this child become bisexual, as both sexes would seem different and exotic?

Or, rather, would a child's dis-identification with both sexes create, at least in some, an ambivalence to both and a sexual disinterest in all people later in life (i.e., asexuality)? This is an intriguing question and perhaps worth pursuing in future research. However, it is important to keep in mind that Bem's theory, even as it applies to typical sexual orientation development, is controversial and lacks direct support. Moreover, it is also important to remember that the causal relationships among these variables could be viewed in the reverse direction: one's attractions may cause the degree to which we identify with our own sex. So, if some asexual people do not identify as male or female, it may be because their lack of sexual attraction makes them feel like they have little in common (or dis-identify) with being male or female, not the other way around. Moreover, in line with this reasoning, as I suggested above, some women's lack of sexual attraction may make them less "feminine," because they are not as socialized to be an object of desire.

SUMMARY

Sex and gender are complex constructs, but they are useful in understanding asexuality. Gender differences in asexuality seem to parallel gender differences in sexuality (e.g., masturbation). We do not know whether asexual people conform to traditional gender roles, although I speculate that asexual people are, on average, less conforming (e.g., asexual women have less object-of-desire self-consciousness). There is a strong suggestion in the current literature that many asexual people do not identify as male or female. The degree to which gender roles and gender identity play a causal role in the sexuality of asexual people is unknown, as is the degree to which asexuality plays a causal role in their gender roles and identities. Finally, I hope you see how exploring asexuality helps us to understand, or at least consider, the complexity of sexuality and the different ways it plays out in men and women. For example, we learn more about that mystery of mysteries—the nature of women's sexuality, particularly the purpose of their non-category-specific responses—by including asexual women in the mix. And who knows—perhaps soon we may even be able to answer Freud's famous query on the nature of women's desires. However, even if we aren't able to answer this question, there is a still a wealth of knowledge to be discovered by exploring the intersection of sex, gender, and asexuality.

NOTE

1. Note that biological and environmental/social explanations are not necessarily incompatible. As suggested in chapter 13, these two kinds of explanations can coexist because they offer different levels of analysis: micro (biological) versus macro (environment/social). Thus, they may represent different points along a causal stream or pathway. For example, a specific biological predisposition may make someone particularly sensitive to a certain environment, which ultimately has a large impact on this person, whereas a different biological predisposition may make another person especially sensitive to a completely different environment, which may also have a large (but different) impact on him or her.

SEVEN

Forging an (A)sexual Identity

There is an Australian children's book called *Miss Lily's Fabulous Pink Feather Boa*. It is about a cute but nearly extinct marsupial, a long-nosed potoroo, trying to locate its place in the world. By the end of the book, the little potoroo discovers—to both its and sympathetic readers' relief—that it is not alone: there is a small band of its kind, with whom it forges lasting and meaningful relationships (Wild & Argent, 1998).

Throughout much of the book, the potoroo wears a pink, feathered boa, which it claims from the eccentric Miss Lily. This rather odd but endearing affectation made me wonder if this book, aside from its main lessons in environmentalism and how to stick it out if you are indeed a lonely little potoroo, is offering another, more subtle message. I wonder if it is meant in an allegorical way to represent the solitary existence and ultimately the "coming out" experience of sexual minorities—particularly gay men, some of whom, of course, have similarly fabulous affectations (Rieger, Linsenmeier, Gygax, & Bailey, 2008).

If you are a heterosexual person, imagine that you are the only one in your school, or at work, or in your extended family who has these attractions to the other sex. All others are attracted to the same sex, or attracted to no one. How would you feel? Perhaps like the little potoroo?

In this chapter, I discuss sexual identity formation—both in sexual people and, in particular, in asexual people. Let's begin by addressing a fundamental question: Why is a sexual identity important to people in the first place? Why does a person need to locate, psychologically speaking, his or her *sexual self*, and perhaps express it, even publicly?

This is not just an interesting question for academic types like me; it is a curious, even burning, question in many laypeople's minds. Some heterosexual people, for example, wonder why gays and lesbians have to "go flaunting their sexualities" all over the place in gay pride festivities. Perhaps there is an implied homophobia to such statements from heterosexual people (i.e., they do not want to be exposed to a sexuality they don't like or are uncomfortable with). Yet I also expect that some heterosexual people just truly wonder what all the fuss is about, because they, as heterosexual people, don't have a parade announcing their sexuality.

Similarly, Dan Savage, an outspoken sex columnist (is there any other kind?), has questioned the need for asexual people to assert their identity, at least within a public sphere (Chevigny, Davenport, Pinder, & Tucker, 2011). He argues that it is clear why gays and lesbians, for example, need to assert their identity in a public sphere. Public announcements and displays of sexual identity are important so that sexual minorities, such as gay men, can claim the right to engage in, in his words, ahem, "cock sucking." Well, what if you are asexual? If you are not engaging in potentially prohibited behavior (e.g., fellatio among men) and thus do not need public acceptance (or at least tolerance) of it, why go out and make public displays of your identity, or demonstrate in a parade or a public march? After all, no one cares that you are *not* having sex, and no one will put you in jail for not having sex. So, what is all the fuss about? Just stay at home when the next gay parade rolls around.

Dan Savage has a point here, and his argument goes some way in answering the above-mentioned query from some heterosexual people about why lesbians and gays go about "flaunting their sexualities" at gay pride parades: they need to achieve acceptance and recognition for potentially prohibited behaviors. Interestingly, this view—that public displays of identity are particularly important for gays and lesbians and perhaps less so for asexuals—is probably not lost, at least on some level, on many asexual people. So while some asexual people do march and assert their identities publicly (Childs, 2009, January 16), I expect that a large number of asexuals quietly go about their lives without ever signing on to a chat-line or a website devoted to asexual issues, let alone joining a march devoted to sexual minorities.

But let's get back to Dan Savage's main point. Although there is some sense in it, I also think it misses a more important, broader point: The relevance of having an identity (and being able to express it) goes beyond gaining acceptance for, and therefore access to, behavior that might otherwise be prohibited. It has to do with answering some basic questions about oneself (e.g., *Who am I? How do I fit in with others?*). It also has to do with expressing oneself and seeking some level of acceptance from others for one's existence (e.g., *I exist, and I want the world to know and recognize that I exist*). Identity formation, including the sexual identity process that is part of the broader identity-formation process, is a fundamental aspect of human development (Lawler, 2008; Leary & Tangney, 2003; Mathews, Bok, & Rabins, 2009). Anyone who knows a teenager, or recalls his or her own teen years, understands how important and fundamental identity formation can be. Similarly, the fact that most societies, cultures, and religious groups have "coming of age" rites attests to the importance of identity formation in human development, particularly within the context of reproductive/sexual maturation. Thus identity issues, sexual and otherwise, are also relevant to asexual people.

Interestingly, identity formation is increasingly relevant to a group whose sexuality may not fit comfortably within either the sexual or the asexual realm. For example, a number of people have migrated to the AVEN website/community who identify themselves as "gray-a." Thus, these individuals feel they fit somewhere on the spectrum between sexual and asexual. This fact also demonstrates the importance of identity formation and people's need to find their place in the world. We all need a language to describe ourselves that reflects our commonalities with those who share our characteristics and our differences from those who don't.

The sexual identity process in asexual people has not been studied extensively, at least not to the extent to which it has been studied in gays and lesbians. But processes similar to those that occur in gays and lesbians are also likely to occur in asexual people, given that there are some similar issues—namely, being a sexual minority in a heterosexual (and heterosexist) world (Scherrer, 2008).

Theorists have argued that there are a variety of stages to sexual identity formation in sexual minorities. One of the first stages is recognizing one's own attractions. Later stages include testing and exploring one's attractions, along with identifying/labeling oneself (e.g., as gay, bisexual, or lesbian). Final stages might potentially include making public disclosures and developing identity pride (Cass, 1979; Coleman, 1982; Floyd & Stein, 2002; Troiden, 1989). When someone is described as "coming out" (e.g., to one's parents), this usually refers to public disclosures, or the formation of a public identity (Cass, 1996). For example, public disclosure is typically how most gay, lesbian, and bisexual people understand "coming out." However, when identity theorists discuss sexual identity formation in sexual minorities, they usually refer to the whole process, and not just coming out. Thus, there is recognition of the complexity and the multiple facets or stages of identity formation. Identity theorists have also recently recognized that discrete steps or stages may not always capture the true phenomenology (i.e., the reality or lived experience) of the sexual identity process in sexual minorities. For example, the so-called stages may blend into one another, or the timing may be reversed for some people. Relatedly, there is a recent suggestion that gays and lesbians can often have different developmental experiences of sexual identity formation (Diamond, 2006; Rust, 1993). Thus, even while current theorists recognize the complexity of people's coming-out experiences and the importance of considering various stages (as a heuristic or learning tool), there is probably a need to make the models even more complex. *Damn those complex humans!*

Despite the limitations, let's assume that these theoretical stages of the sexual identity process have heuristic value. Let's also assume that they are relevant, at least to some degree, to an asexual person in forging his or her sexual identity.

As mentioned, one of the stages of the identity process can be coming out, or the making of public disclosures. What makes a person come out sooner rather than later, or perhaps never come out at all? There are a variety of factors that have been associated with an early (versus a later) coming-out experience, including one's age or, more accurately, the era into which one was born. Younger cohorts of gays and lesbians come out sooner than older cohorts, at least in Western society (Floyd & Bakeman, 2006). This trend may say something about the changing state of Western society, particularly the increasing degree of acceptance of sexual minorities relative to past eras.

My colleague Carolyn Hafer and I discovered that beliefs about the world are also important in the timing of coming out (Bogaert & Hafer, 2009). When gay men believe that the world is just—that people get what they deserve and deserve what they get (Lerner, 1980)—they are more likely to come out sooner, as opposed to those who don't hold these beliefs. In contrast, gay men who believe that the world is unjust, relative to those who believe that the world is just, are more likely to stay in the closet until later in life (or not come out at all).[1] We speculated that beliefs about the justice of the world are important in gay men's coming-out experience because gay men are often the subjects of discrimination (Herek, 2000; Herek, 2002). Thus, believing that the world that awaits you is full of injustices, and that those injustices will be directed at you in the form of discrimination—sometimes an accurate perception—can make one shy away from making a grand entrance onto the world's stage. There is a saying that "justice delayed is justice denied." This research suggests a modified version of this maxim: "an entrance delayed is an injustice denied" (or so some gay people may perceive the situation).

Do asexual people also delay their coming-out experiences for fear of public reprisals, believing that the world will be unjust to them? It is hard to know at this point, because there is no research on the issue. I expect, however, that some probably do, given that most asexual people likely believe that they will be perceived with some level of public disdain when they come out. In fact, I expect that a portion of the public do perceive asexual people to be very unusual and bizarre—in short, "freaks." For example, although some of the heterosexual majority may have ambivalence toward gays and lesbians, gays and lesbians are, like heterosexual people, interested in sex. In contrast, asexual people may seem especially foreign to average (heterosexual) people. It is clear from some of my media appearances (e.g., on talk or radio phone-in shows) that some members of the general public do indeed hold these views and are not afraid to espouse them publicly. There is also some recent evidence that asexual people may, in fact, be viewed more negatively than gays, bisexuals, and lesbians—specifically, as "less than human" (see more in chapter 4) (MacInnis & Hodson, in press).

However, some asexual people may not fear public reprisals with the same intensity as gays and lesbians, because they sense that the discrimination against them may be less virulent than what can occur against gays and lesbians. For example, homosexual men are sometimes the victims of "gay bashing" (Berrill, 1992; Federal Bureau of Investigation, 2002). Indeed, the vitriol directed against asexual people may never reach the same intensity as that which has historically been directed against gay men, partially because asexual people probably do not challenge the gender-role expectations of heterosexual men in the same way that gay men do. Some heterosexual men view the effeminacy of some gay men with particular disdain, yet there is no direct evidence of elevated effeminacy in asexual men (but see more on gender in chapter 6). Gender nonconformity likely plays a role in some gay men's fears of coming out, as we discovered that effeminate gay men who believe that the world is unjust are especially likely to delay the coming-out process (Bogaert & Hafer, 2009).

Let's consider some other unique features of asexual development that may contribute to differences in coming-out experiences between asexual people and gays/lesbians. One is the degree of newness of the "asexual" label/identity; after all, asexual identities are likely very recent phenomena (see also chapter 3). A related one is the diffuse nature of the asexual community; recall that asexual people comprise a diverse bunch (see, for example, chapter 5). These features may delay the coming-out experience in asexual people. For example, one asexual woman I met did not come out until her twenties because she just didn't know "what" she was until recently. This makes sense: How can one go through the identity process (including coming out) when there is no obvious group with whom to identify? Recall that labeling oneself (e.g., as "gay") usually comes before, and is arguably a necessary precursor to, coming out (Cass, 1979; Coleman, 1982; Troiden, 1989). After all, one needs a recognizable group, with a label, with whom to identify and of which to come out as a member. Until very recently, there has been no organized and publicly identifiable asexual group. In contrast, gays and lesbians have had a visible and identifiable presence in the Western world for many years, arguably for at least thirty years or more (e.g., Terry, 1999). Of course, despite this fact, some gays and lesbians also may not know their sexual identities until later in life. However, I expect that young people with emerging same-sex attractions have much better access to information on gay and lesbian identities and cultures than young people without any sexual attractions have on asexual identities and cultures.

There is support for the reasoning that asexual people may come out later (or not at all) because there has not been, until recently, a visible group with whom to identify. Bisexuals have more identity confusion and come out later than gays and lesbians, and it has been argued that this difference occurs because there is a less visible and organized bisexual community relative to the gay and lesbian community (Fox, 1995).

Another unique feature of asexual development that may affect public disclosures and coming out in asexual people, relative to gays and les-

bians, was mentioned earlier: lack of sexual behavior does not need legiti-
mizing in the same way as same-sex behavior (e.g., fellatio among men).
After all, no one was ever caught *not engaging in sex* and then put in
prison for it. Asexual people, then, may have a reduced need to come out,
or at least a reduced need for public displays of their sexual orientation,
as there is less of a need to defend their behavior. Indeed, one might
argue that the emergence of the gay/lesbian community as a social force
occurred, at least partly, to secure this legitimacy from the heterosexual
majority and the politicians who serve them. Relatedly, one might also
argue that a coherent and integrated sexual identity in gays and lesbians
was also born of this necessity, in order to allow the group to fight for
their rights as unique sexual beings and to engage freely in sex in the
manner of their choosing. In short, it is important to recognize that (sexual) identities may also emerge out of and serve political and social goals.
Note that I am not implying that a gay/lesbian identity was consciously
created by gay and lesbian political activists, although such activism may
have contributed to this identity; broad social forces also might have
acted to bring these identities to the fore (Terry, 1999). Interestingly, the
military understands these processes and political/social forces. They use
young people's search for an identity and their need to belong (e.g., *You
are a Marine!*) to achieve similar but more extreme social/political effects
during basic training: to motivate and ready soldiers for battle (Dyer,
1985).

If asexual people have less need for battle against oppressive forces in
society (relative to gays and lesbians), this may also partly explain why
they have been unrecognized as a social group, and why a coherent asexual identity and culture has not emerged until recently. Asexual identities and group cohesion among asexual people are not necessities for
many asexual people, as asexual behavior is not at stake if they don't rail
against "the man." In contrast, historically, gay and lesbian people
needed to—and often still need to—rail against the (heterosexual) man to
ensure that they could engage in the sexual behavior of their choosing.

It is also true that sexuality, by definition, is a *nonissue*—off the radar,
so to speak—for many asexual people (Scherrer, 2008). Thus, an asexual
person's need to assert an identity, particularly a public one, may have
little "sexual" slant to it. This is in contrast to gays and lesbians, whose
identity may be more sexualized. After all, sexuality is anything but a
nonissue for them. Indeed, it is relevant and salient to their identities in

two basic ways. First, gay people's sexuality contrasts starkly with the heterosexual majority. Second, like heterosexual people, gays and lesbians are sexual beings, strongly influenced by their desires and attractions. Thus, their sexuality is doubly relevant and likely acts as a creative force in forging their identities. Of course, asexual people share with gays and lesbians their status as a sexual minority, and thus they also stand in contrast to a sexual majority. So, sexuality is potentially important to their identity also, as it makes them stand apart from the majority group. But unlike gays and lesbians, asexual people are not sexual beings (e.g., lacking in sexual attraction), and so sexuality, given that it is a *nonissue*, is not as likely to invade their psychic space and to take front and center position when their identities are being formed.

Consider this quote from an asexual person: "Outside of AVEN or conversations specifically about sexuality, I don't really consciously think of myself as asexual. Like being an atheist or non-Hispanic or a non-driver (all apply), asexuality is something I'm not and never was, rather than something I am. The label is mostly a useful marker. So, my asexual identity is important in certain contexts, and I can't imagine my life if I weren't asexual, but it is not specifically important to me" (Scherrer, 2008, p. 630).

The famous psychologist George Kelly and his personal construct theory are relevant to the two points made above. According to Kelly (1955), the way we see the world, other people, and ourselves is based on our personal constructs. We are construct "constructors." These constructs (or ideas about the way things work) almost always are perceived to have extreme points. Thus, we tend to think about people as occupying an extreme of say, a "happy-sad" dimension: *Sally is happy; Frank is sad*. Thus, the happy-sad construct is defined for us in large part by its extremes. It is not surprising, then, that sexual minorities use extremes, or contrasts, of sexuality (e.g., hetero-homo) to define themselves as people, or that heterosexual people would use these extremes/contrasts in defining sexual minorities. But it is also true that some constructs are just not as relevant for people as other constructs. So, if sexuality is completely removed from one's life (and one barely gives it a second thought), it may not be a personally relevant construct in defining oneself, or in forging one's identity. Some asexual people, then, may have little to no incentive to form an asexual identity and come out, or at least no incentive to make public displays of their nonsexuality.

Consider an example to illustrate this point further: Do non-golfers — *a*golfers?—go to golf courses and march on the eighteenth green to assert their non-golfing identity? It would be rather strange, of course, for non-golfers to do so, because golfing, as an activity and as a construct, is not personally relevant to most of them, nor is it part of their identity. Thus, as a golfer, as I am finishing up my round and heading to the clubhouse, I rarely see such displays and marches from non-golfers.[2]

From the above, it may seem like there are only modest reasons for asexual people to forge and fiercely defend a sexual identity. But we must not discount the importance of the other identity-relevant forces in asexual people's lives, such as general identity needs, not wanting to be alone and isolated, and perceiving oneself on the extreme end of an often very salient construct in society—sexuality. Moreover, there is another reason why forging an identity, developing an asexual culture, and becoming part of a cohesive group is of importance to asexual people: to defend their lives against modern medicalization and the perception that they have a disorder or are unhappy.

But before we address the issue of medicalization, let's consider a little background. Asexuality, broadly defined, has often not been viewed across cultures and historically as a disorder or an illness. In fact, from a religious perspective, asexuality (or at least abstinence) has often been viewed as a virtue. For example, most religions across the world proscribe liberal sexuality, and some (e.g., Buddhism, Roman Catholicism) still view abstinence as a virtue. Moreover, non-religiously based institutions, including the Western medical establishment, historically would not likely have labeled asexuality a disorder, particularly in women. In the 1950s and 1960s, this started to change. Sexuality became decoupled from reproduction, and sex was viewed on its own merits; that is, as a source of physical pleasure, recreation, and so forth (Sigusch, 1998).

Given this decoupling of sex from reproduction, it is perhaps understandable that the absence of sexuality started to be seen as a potential problem and eventually found its way into important medical texts and manuals, like the *Diagnostic and Statistical Manual of Mental Disorders* (*DSM-III*) (American Psychiatric Association, 1980). (Most North American clinicians diagnose mental health problems based on criteria found in the *DSM*.) For example, "inhibited sexual desire," a name later changed to "hypoactive sexual desire disorder," first appeared in this manual in 1980. About ten years later, "lack or loss of sexual desire" first

appeared in another important medical manual, the *International Statistical Classification of Diseases and Related Health Problems* *(ICD-10)* (World
Health Organization, 1992). Some social critics, particularly feminists,
have also argued that the medicalization of many aspects of sexuality,
including asexuality—again, broadly defined—has occurred because
there are profits to be had from creating disorders where, arguably, none
existed before (Drew, 2003; Fishman, 2004; Fishman, 2007; Tiefer, 2002).

In the wake of this medicalization of asexuality, the modern asexuality movement began. David Jay, the founding member of the most popular asexuality website, AVEN, has explained at various times why he
began the site. His reasons seem to reflect a number of the identity issues
mentioned above. For example, one reason was personal: "He was driven
by memories of feeling alone. As a teenager in St. Louis, he searched the
Web for *asexual* and found only research on amoebas" (Bulwa, 2009, August 24). Another reason was educational—to help other asexual people
understand more about themselves (Bulwa, 2009, August 24). Indeed,
there are various stories of asexual people "discovering themselves"
through AVEN. For example, one young woman recalls that AVEN "described her so accurately . . . that she cried over her keyboard" (Bulwa,
2009, August 24).

It is also clear that, over time, Jay wanted to build a community that
would enable asexual people to change the way the world (especially the
medical world) views them. Thus, this last reason for developing AVEN
is in line with (public) identities being a means of social and political
change. He has said, "When I was younger, the message I would always
hear is that you need sex to be happy" (Childs, 2009, January 16). He has
also said, "We need to know we're not broken" (Bulwa, 2009, August 24),
and "We need to have more discussion about how people can not have
sex and still be happy" (Childs, 2009, January 16). This last reason for
founding and expanding AVEN has led to an active movement to do just
that: Some AVEN members have become a vocal group lobbying to
change the way the latest *DSM* edition labels asexual people, particularly
if they are not distressed about their lack of sexual interest/attraction.
One media report stated this directly: "AVEN members have one con-
crete goal: changing the authoritative *Diagnostic and Statistical Manual of
Mental Disorders* to make explicit that asexuality is not a hypoactive sexual desire disorder" (Bulwa, 2009, August 24). However, such change begins with, or at least is facilitated by, a cohesive group rallying around a

relevant identity or common label. After all, having an identity as an "asexual" person has its benefits, both personally and politically. In the recent scientific and clinical literature, the words most widely used to describe asexual people have intimated, if not actively embraced, the language of illness and disease (e.g., "hypoactive sexual desire disorder"). In contrast, the word "asexual" is merely descriptive of the phenomenon and not laden with values; it does not imply that a specific level of sexual interest or attraction is correct and healthy. Thus, people who embrace the identity of an "asexual" are likely more positive about their self-image than those who are asexual but do not identify as such, and particularly relative to those who use medical or clinical language to describe themselves. People who embrace an identity as "asexual" are also, I expect, more likely to form a cohesive political group than those who do not identify as such and/or those who choose more medical or clinical language to describe themselves. Embracing an asexual identity also, in turn, potentially enables asexual people to change the medical establishment, or at least its rules for what is and what is not a mental illness. And they may succeed in doing so.

SUMMARY

Identities allow us to know who we are and to stake our claim as unique and worthy of recognition. They also allow us to seek solace and comfort with, and forge ties to, those with whom we share commonalities. Identities also often emerge out of and serve social and political ends, allowing us to rally our group in defense of our interests.

Sexual identities are especially powerful components of the broader human identity process. That many asexual people still want, or are compelled, to forge a sexual identity (i.e., as an *asexual*) attests to the relevance and power of sex in our society. They are, like the potoroo, seemingly alone in a very large and different (sexual) world. Sexuality is also likely to be, at least for some, a very relevant personal construct, even if they do not engage in sex at all. It is as if these asexuals know that, on some very deep level, sex really matters in society, and therefore their own identities must also be defined by it, even if that identification takes on meaning because it is the polar opposite of sex. An asexual identity is also clearly relevant from a political standpoint, providing the ground support and a rallying point needed to change public perceptions and institutions that claim (or at least imply) that asexual people are ill or broken. That (public) identities are often political, and can serve as a way of gaining or defending psychic and other territory, is illustrated by the fact that groups often tend to lose their (unique) identity when the "war" is over and won (Associated Press, 2007; Scarr, 1987). For example, some recent stories on the gay and lesbian community illustrate how traditional elements of a gay/lesbian identity are being lost in the wake of increasing public acceptance. For asexual people, however, their war—and their need for a common identity to help fight it—has probably just begun.

NOTES

1. We are currently collecting data on the coming-out process in lesbians and bisexual women, and it will be interesting to see if we can replicate these findings in women. In our first study (Bogaert and Hafer, 2009), there was not a sufficiently large sample to test this issue in women.

2. As mentioned, I have a thing for golf; thus, golfing examples clearly have a special resonance for me.

EIGHT

The Madness of Sex

One day in the locker room I overheard a conversation between a gregarious old man and his younger male friend. The conversation flitted among seemingly unrelated topics, but eventually landed on one that seemed to pique the old man's interest more than others. He described, with some curiosity, how his interests in sex had changed: It no longer appealed. As an example, he noted that, these days, the famous and staggeringly popular *Sports Illustrated* swimsuit issue, sent to him as part of his regular subscription to this magazine, was "wasted." The bathing beauties (meant to remind avid sports fans that there was, after all, one additional, equally important reason to live) were just a bit of an oddity to him. They "did nothing" for him. He concluded, to his own amusement, that perhaps if these women were carrying a steaming-hot pepperoni pizza, then maybe they would pique his interest!

Most sexual people have an understanding of this old man's feelings. Sexual people can go through periods in their lives when sex holds little interest for them. Perhaps a stressful job, a tough bit of schooling, or a family tragedy is the cause of these relatively transitory bouts of sexual disinterest. And, of course, on a shorter time scale, in any given day, people have periods when sex—even if the opportunity presents itself to have sex with an attractive partner—is not appealing, or at least not uppermost in one's thoughts. We are routinely occupied by the day-to-day realities of life, and sex may seem very unappealing (or even a bit alien) at any given moment. Even average adolescent males or young men, whose sex drives are said to be like an endless well, have a "refractory period," which refers to a state of disinterest (or no arousal) after sex.

In such relatively sexless states, one's higher-order, analytical thinking may hold sway, and thus one may wonder what all the fuss is about (see also chapter 1): Why is sex such an important and powerful influence in one's life? One may even have a curious feeling—an *aha!* moment—that sex, if the truth be told, is a curious, even peculiar, activity and preoccupation. At such times, one has caught a glimpse of what I call the *madness of sex*. You could also call it, perhaps, an asexual's perspective on human sexuality.

Incidentally, I knew a college professor who called adolescence the state of "testosterone poisoning." He was trying to be funny, of course, but his description of adolescence also captures the same underlying idea here: that the activities of, and preoccupation with, sex (along with the hormone that provides some of the motivation for it, testosterone) can be seen as a kind of odd—even mad—state of mind. And certainly, as mentioned in chapter 1, if one views sex from a distance ("deconstructs" it, if you will), it can be seen as comprising a host of symptom-like behaviors—obsessive thoughts, odd vocalizations, repetitive movements, and so on—reminiscent of a mental disorder.

Most, if not all, sexual people, then, may have some understanding of what it would be like to be asexual *all the time*. They might even wonder whether asexual people have a special knowledge, seeing sex for what it truly is: a rather strange preoccupation partly induced by a brain poison (i.e., hormones). Prepubescent children (i.e., before their hormonal surge) often have this view of sex, wondering *why* in heaven's name would someone want to do *that*, as if it were as sensible and pleasurable as repeatedly sticking one's finger in another's ear. Perhaps prepubescence can be construed as a form of asexuality or, more accurately, as a related phenomenon: presexuality.

On the AVEN website, comments at times appear about the strange, nonsensical activities of sexual people. I hear that AVEN webmasters sometimes have to rein in some of the more extreme and disparaging comments on these strange activities of sexual people. It reminds me of the disparaging rant that some gay people hurl at heterosexuals: *Breeders!* I suppose this comment is meant to suggest that the heterosexual habit of overpopulating a fragile planet with their offspring is, well, a bit self-centered and gauche. Both views have merit perhaps, and maybe there are webmasters reining in breeder rants on gay/lesbian sites as well.

The view that sex is odd is sometimes afforded to people when exposed to sexual activities that they don't find stimulating. Heterosexual men, for example, may find gay porn to be curious, even amusing, rather than titillating or deeply arousing. When they watch it, they may feel like an observer watching someone sticking a probe into a friend's ear, and although it is clear that both the prober and the one being probed find (or feign) this activity deeply interesting and satisfying (e.g., by their vocalizations or other telltale signs), the heterosexual viewer may feel that there is no apparent reason for this activity. Thus, they are left with a largely curious, even amused reaction. There is a scene in the movie *The Kids Are Alright* in which a lesbian couple is turned on by gay (male) porn and incorporates it into their lovemaking (Gilbert et al., 2010). The movie shows snippets of a gay porn movie, but the sex scenes are played up in such a way as to seem amusing. I think the filmmakers were playfully suggesting, perhaps in line with the themes of the movie, that any sex is a bit odd (regardless of the players) and can be viewed with curious amusement when seen from the outsider's perspective. It just so happens that the viewers (in the audience) are likely predominantly heterosexual, as they are the majority in society, but it could be the other way around: gay people viewing heterosexual porn—or, more to the point, asexual people viewing any porn (but see chapter 10).

Even while in the throes of sexual acts themselves, sexual people may have some understanding of the feverish madness of sex. Thus, if a heterosexual woman has an exciting new sexual partner and he is nearly all-consuming for her, she may still have, in moments of reflection, some knowledge of how her recent life has turned upside down because of him. An even more extreme example is a married heterosexual man who spends an inordinate amount of time and money on prostitutes. Yet on some level he "knows" that his behavior is irrational. He may even know that he is on the verge of ruining his life, as his job and family life are at stake. Some clinicians, of course, call this kind of sexual behavior an addiction.

Sometimes the madness of sex has little to do with actual behaviors, and more to do with a fantasy that never gets lived out because the object of desire is unattainable. Thus a classmate or colleague at work becomes an obsession; a carefully managed fantasy, perhaps, but at weaker moments the fantasy may leak into, and even disrupt, an otherwise tranquil home life.

I have a very vivid memory of an incident like this on a beach in Australia. I was nestled on a blanket watching the surf, the sand, and the people, when I noted this man, his wife, and their three children making their way onto the beach. They seemed like an average family (if such a thing exists), looking to secure for themselves a bit of beach real estate. Aside from this preoccupation, the man was caught up by the details of his family life, which, it seemed, was not going well this morning and was spilling over, rather noisily, onto the beach. His wife was imploring him to tend to a nagging child complaining about an older sibling, who was, it seemed, a bit of a hitter. The man looked frazzled, haggard, even old, although I bet he wasn't a day over thirty. Just then, as if he had been doused by cold water, he stopped, and his jaw dropped like a lead weight, because he noticed a topless sunbathing woman—in fact, he almost stepped on her. Evidently, in his eyes, she was gorgeous. His stare was of a man completely taken in—lost, in fact. And you could see that, at that moment, if she got up from her towel and went up to him and asked him if he wanted to spend the night together, he would have chosen to do so eagerly, whatever the consequences to his marriage and family. Clearly, so much of the power—and the madness—of sex are in its possibility, not its actuality. Of course, people often try to keep the madness of sex in check, relegating it to their fantasies, but it is still madness. The Australian story is, of course, a testament to the agony of the wanted but unattainable.

Aside from these anecdotal examples, there is scientific research to support my view on the madness of sex. Indeed, research evidence suggests that people's cognitive functioning is impaired significantly when preoccupied with sex, even if they are not in the heat of a sexual moment. Heterosexual men primed to think of potential sexual activities (via pictures of beautiful women, fully clothed) have a diminished capacity for a type of rational thought—the ability to plan well for the future (Wilson & Daly, 2004). That is, they "discount" the future. It is as if the future becomes a less-than-plausible reality in the wake of the sexually charged moment. The researchers speculate that the possibility of mating (even if it is an unrealistic prospect, as the men knew they were never going to meet the women) makes men's minds become too focused on the "mating moment," as if the future does not matter. The researchers argue that the images of attractive women affect the brain—exciting nerve centers associated with mating, and shutting down more rational, planning-oriented centers—in a similar way as the prospect of real mating. When human brains evolved hundreds of thousands of years ago, there were, of course, no photographs. So, these modern two-dimensional images trick men's Stone Age minds into responding as if there were actually beautiful women smiling in front of them. The men's response, then, is doubly irrational: first, they are responding to pictures as if they were reality (no, boys, a real woman has not just *beamed* into your bedrooms!), and second, they are discounting the future at the prospect of sex.

One could argue that, from a gene-based view of life, the second irrationality—discounting the future at the prospect of sex—does make some "sense," as the future doesn't amount to a hill of beans if there is great potential right now to mate and replicate one's genes. After all, the future is only important if the genetic payoff down the road is plausibly greater than the genetic payoff in the here and now. From this perspective, the "future" (i.e., a long life with plans, schemes, and delays of gratification) only exists as a concept in our minds because it often leads to genetic payoffs. Even so, let's not forget the main point here: Isn't it bizarre (and mad!) that the prospect of sex—and a mere image, no less—has the capacity to derail the best laid plans of mice and (particularly) men?[1]

There are other studies showing that sex is linked to various "unhealthy" behaviors (taking physical risks, exposure to infectious diseases, etc.). One study showed that adolescent boys and young men were more likely to take physical risks (e.g., doing crazy tricks) when skateboarding in the presence of an attractive woman, and this effect was caused by elevated testosterone (Ronay & von Hippel, 2010), the hormonal "poison" mentioned earlier. There is also a recent study showing that when women are primed (e.g., given very brief glimpses or reminders) with romantic and sexual themes, they have an increased willingness to engage in unhealthy and risky behaviors, like using risky dieting pills and going to cancer-causing tanning salons (Hill & Durante, 2011). The authors of the study also found that the women felt a diminished sense of vulnerability when mating goals are uppermost in their minds.

People think that our attitudes are rationally formed, the result of well-thought-out arguments and an astute and sensitive scaling of the pros and cons of the issues, along with, of course, accumulated wisdom from years of experience. Yet our attitudes are frequently governed by irrational, emotional states including—yes, you guessed it!—sexual desires. An example: One of the reasons that heterosexual men have negative attitudes toward male homosexuality but not female homosexuality is sexual in nature. Heterosexual men are often turned on by lesbian sex (Louderback & Whitley, 1997), and if one takes this arousal away, heterosexual men's positive attitude toward lesbianism no longer exists. So, a little sexual desire/arousal toward lesbianism, and presto: positive (or at least neutral) attitudes toward it! After all, how could lesbian sex be wrong, immoral, and disgusting, if I am turned on by it? Impossible!

Ever flown into a jealous rage—just "lost it"—over a partner's flirtation or outright sexual indiscretion with another? Most adults have experienced sexual jealousy, along with the torturous effects this emotion has on one's thoughts and plans, even if the emotion itself doesn't disintegrate into extreme behavior. But sometimes it does: sexual jealousy is considered one of the main motives in killings that occur in domestic disputes within the United States (Daly & Wilson, 1988; Daly, Wilson, & Weghorst, 1982). When a jealous rage does descend into violence, the resulting act is sometimes called a crime of passion. In civil courts in the United States, crimes of passion can be defensible if one pleads "temporary insanity," making the defendant (at least theoretically) no longer criminally liable. Similarly, in nineteenth-century France, a *crime passionnel* (or crime of passion), including murder, was defensible in the same way. The fact that the courts in various societies at various time periods recognize that sex, at least under certain circumstances, causes "insanity" illustrates my main point: sex, in many manifestations, and perhaps even at its core, is mad.

When liberal-minded observers hear about the sex scandal of a celebrity (e.g., David Letterman) or a sports personality (e.g., Tiger Woods) or a politician (e.g., Bill Clinton, Arnold Schwarzenegger, Dominique Strauss-Kahn), they typically do not decry what might be perceived by more conservative observers to be the shocking immorality of the acts, but rather the shocking stupidity of the perpetrator's behavior in getting caught. And it is clear that there is at times an almost wanton disregard for any kind of careful planning or thoughtful execution in relation to behaviors that, if discovered, could do serious damage to their reputations and careers. Even more telling is that many of the people caught in such scandals are incredibly bright, savvy, and highly functioning in the social sphere.

One might argue that this wanton behavior has less to do with the maddening effects of sex, and more to do with a sense of entitlement and disregard for others that seems to go hand in hand with power, status, and narcissism. Partly true, I expect, but this is likely not the whole story. For example, it does not explain the often careful and thoughtful behavior these men routinely display in other areas of their lives. If behavior in these other domains were chosen carelessly, it could be almost as damaging to their careers as an awkwardly planned sexual liaison. In addition, if one prefers a "power explanation" over a "sex explanation" to account for this wanton behavior of men of celebrity and status, one would still have to account for the tricky interplay of power and sex, particularly in men. For example, there is a surge of testosterone (potentially affecting both sex drive and feelings of power) in men after they win at competitions (Carré, Putnam, & McCormick, 2009). In short, it is very difficult to disentangle power from many men's sexual motives (and vice versa). It is also hard to argue that sex is not at least partly the culprit underlying the seeming irrationality of the behavior leading to these scandals.

There is an antidrug ad showing an egg sizzling in a frying pan. The caption reads, "This is your brain on drugs." Perhaps an equivalent one should be reserved for sex ("This is your brain on sex"), since brains on sex, including the brains of celebrities, politicians, and sports figures, do irrational things.

Three months after his bizarre car crash and a myriad of rumors, Tiger Woods[2] emerged on February 19, 2010, from his public hibernation to offer a *mea culpa* for his extramarital affairs and their impact on his family, friends, fellow players, fans, and sponsors. One of the more interesting elements of all this was the astonishing degree of interest in this story, relative to all the other issues of the day. One newspaper headline asserted boldly, "The world stops for 13 minutes" (Broad, 2010, February 28). Not literally true, of course, but almost: the New York Stock Exchange did stop trading for the thirteen minutes to watch the spectacle of Woods's carefully crafted news conference. "Tiger Woods News Conference" was also the highest-rated Google search term by midday. The level of interest in this story, as with the scandals before and after it, was driven by sexual curiosity. This is not to say that there weren't other angles that made people curious to watch or to hear or to read about it (e.g., the business/sponsorship impact), but the only angle that drove it to this level of fury was clearly the sexual one.

Also, consider this: the fact that a relatively conservative, business-oriented newspaper—Canada's *The Globe and Mail*—would say that the "world stopped" (Broad, 2010, February 28) illustrates a main point of this book, that one's view of the world—including the perception of whether it seems to stop or seems to run at a breakneck pace—is filtered through the different lenses that we have for seeing it. Most people see the world through sexual lenses, just as business-oriented people often see the world through business-oriented lenses; the lenses we wear—sexual or otherwise—are often no longer obvious to us, just as a long-worn set of spectacles over the years becomes imperceptible to the wearer and may even feel like part of his or her own face.

What much of the public and the media did not realize was that Woods's apology was borne out of his need to complete a number of essential "steps" in his "sexual addiction" treatment, similar to the thera-peutic steps required in Alcoholics Anonymous. These steps include an apology to all those whom his sexually addictive behavior (and its seque-lae) has wronged in one way or another. It is perhaps fitting that it came in the form of a highly rated press conference, which was meant to reach not just family and friends but also fellow golfers, his fans, and sponsors, because the scandal and fallout probably affected—rightly or wrongly—many millions of people.[3]

One of the interesting elements of this episode, however, was the fact that part of the public and much of the press wanted Woods to have a public shaming. They seemed to want him to admit that his sense of entitlement led to arguably excessive sexual behavior—including, evi-dently, threesomes with prostitutes. But why was this sexual shaming necessary, or at least interesting to us? Is it because sex is embedded, even pathologically so, in our culture and in the way we think?

But let's push the point further by turning it on its head. Why is it that Tiger Woods's sense of entitlement should not have spurred a public apology, a shaming, over his other excesses, ones that are arguably much more harmful to the planet and humanity than his sexual ones? Why isn't he apologizing for his egregious and excessive consumption of the world's resources and pollution of the planet? Why isn't he apologizing for his private jet, his gas-guzzling vehicles, and the energy consumption in his houses, which could otherwise run a small country? (That is also an interesting "threesome," by the way.) More importantly, why aren't we more interested in that apology, rather than the one we got? Why wouldn't the world stop for thirteen minutes for that? I think you know the answer: *Because it is not about sex, and people are mad about sex.*[4]

SUMMARY

Sex is *the* great story of life (see chapter 1), but it is also truly and utterly mad. Some might argue that, yes, it is mad, but it does not have to be so. It is our culture that makes it mad, and if we were to strip away the neuroticism and hypocrisy from it and "raise the children right," it would not be so. Whether this is true or not, it is an interesting argument to consider. What definitely is true is that the current state of sex should make us cautious about assuming that the absence of sex in one form or another—asexuality—is pathological. I discuss this subject—whether asexuality is indeed a disorder—more fully in my next chapter.

NOTES

1. Yes, I am taking liberties with John Steinbeck's famous book title.
2. This section on Tiger Woods reopened a wound for me and was a bit difficult to write. Ever since I turned forty, I have been obsessed with golf, a game I played in my childhood, let slide in my twenties and thirties, and then recently returned to. So, since midlife, I have played a lot of golf and watched a ton of it on TV. My obsession reflects, perhaps, a bit of the energy of a midlife crisis channeled into this (harmless?) indulgence. Thus, I think I have used golf as an escape from my regular work life as a sexologist, which, of course, was filled with sex. Basically, I needed an escape, and golf was a good one, as it was totally removed from sex. Is there anything less sexy than golf? (Maybe a few things, but not many.) However, after the Tiger Woods sex scandal, my two worlds—sex and golf—collided, and now I can't play golf, or watch it on TV, in the same way. Alas.
3. The paragraph above is not meant to imply that I believe such a public apology was necessary, either from a therapeutic perspective or because it was morally right to do so given his behavior. It is also not meant to imply that I believe that Tiger Woods has an "addiction," which, by the way, many sexologists believe is not an appropriate name for sexual problems. I am also not necessarily implying he had a "sexual problem." (Given his cover-up of his affairs to his wife and her reaction to them when they were revealed, however, it is clear to me that he had a relationship problem.) Rather, this story is merely meant to give a context for why this event occurred.
4. I am picking on Tiger Woods about his excessive use of the world's resources, but I could have chosen countless examples of excessive resource use in people, including myself, whose middle-class Western lifestyle (including my golf) is also open to criticism.

NINE

Do You Have Hypoactive Skydiving Disorder?

Is there only one right way to live a human life? Must people have certain experiences to make their lives worthwhile and healthy? Most of us grapple with these kinds of questions, as they help us to understand our goals, setbacks, and achievements in life. I've also grappled with these questions from an academic perspective, because I was (and still am) trying to understand whether asexuality should be considered a disorder (Bogaert, 2006b). This is the subject of the present chapter. I examine whether asexuality should be seen as unhealthy, and I do so from a number of different perspectives; in other words, I try to put on a number of different lenses and see what I can see.

From one perspective, we might argue that asexuality is a disorder because it goes against life's natural order of things; after all, sex is a natural process, and the desire to "do it" with others is what all (sexual) life strives to do in one form or another. This view of asexuality as disorder uses a lens crafted by evolutionary biology. Thus, asexuality (i.e., a lack of sexual attraction) may seem to contradict an important biological imperative: sex is the means by which humans reproduce, and thus to eschew this aspect of life may seem to fail at a basic goal of life—to reproduce.

When an organism reproduces, its genes are passed on to future generations. The "winners," or the best-adapted organisms, are the ones that pass on the most genes to future generations. The most maladapted are the ones that don't pass on genes (or that pass on the fewest genes) to future generations. Most human beings do the replication game, or attempt to do this, through *sexual* reproduction. Thus a sexual interest in the opposite sex—as the means of reproduction—should be considered a normal and healthy preoccupation. So, for instance, let's consider a fictional person—we'll call her "Sally"—who lived between 1920 and 2000. She married and had three children, two of whom also had children. Thus, her genes have been passed on to future generations through her children (and grandchildren), conceived through a traditional heterosexual relationship. The psychological mechanisms that allowed her to accomplish this were fairly traditional: she was sexually and romantically attracted to men, and had a desire and ability to nurture children. Thus, her tendencies to adopt a traditional heterosexual relationship, along with her nurturance and intelligence as a parent, allowed her to conceive, give birth to, and ultimately raise three vehicles to her genetic posterity (i.e., three kids). Way to go, Sally! Or, perhaps more accurately, way to go, Sally's genes!

From this perspective, individuals having these tendencies to replicate their genes through sexual reproduction are perhaps "healthy," the reasoning goes, because they conform to a natural process that all successful (sexual) life forms follow.

But let's consider some complications with this perspective. First, many sexual people (even a few heterosexual biologists I know) do not have children—including many who do not forgo the mechanism of reproduction itself, sex—and thus fail miserably on this ultimate of biological imperatives. So, do they have a *disorder* or are they *unhealthy*?

Second, there is more than one way to skin a cat, evolutionarily speaking. As suggested in chapter 3, the replication of DNA does occur via asexual reproduction in a host of organisms. So, sexual reproduction is not the *only* natural process of reproduction. Moreover, aside from asexual reproduction occurring in simpler or phylogenetically older species, sexual reproduction is not the only game in town in other, more complex or recently evolved species—even in human beings! Individuals can potentially replicate their genes through other means than sexual reproduction—in particular, via *kin-selection* processes. In these processes, the replication of one's genes occurs through kin or closely related relatives. Our relatives share our genes, and the closer the blood relation (e.g., brother or sister as compared to third cousin), the more genes in common. Thus, if our relatives replicate their genes (through, for example, sexual reproduction), we replicate ours, because a portion of their genes is, in fact, a portion of our genes. Kin-selection mechanisms are also adaptive ("healthy," if you will) alternative strategies to replicate genes. So, even though sexual reproduction is probably the primary method by which human beings replicate their genes, it is not the only way gene replication can occur.

This kin-selection model of gene replication may provide an important answer to why homosexuality exists in humans. On the surface, homosexuality is a challenge to evolutionary types (e.g., biologists, evolutionary psychologists): Gay people don't do sexual reproduction—or at least not to the extent that heterosexual people do—yet homosexuality has existed over time and across cultures and seems to have, at least partially, a genetic basis (Bailey, Dunne, & Martin, 2000; Hamer, Hu, Magnuson, Hu, & Pattatucci, 1993). So, how could "gay genes" ever compete with "straight genes," if the latter find themselves in a group (i.e., breeders) that engages in sexual reproduction, whereas the former find themselves in a group that, on average, doesn't?[1]

The answer may have to do with the kin of gay people. If a gay gene confers some kind of reproductive advantage when expressed in the relatives of gay people, then the gay gene could survive, even flourish, throughout evolutionary history. Recently, researchers have found evidence that gay men have female relatives who are especially fecund, tending to have a lot of children (Iemmola & Camperio-Ciani, 2009). Aha! So, even though gay men don't breed like their heterosexual male counterparts do, their sisters may do so, and at a high rate relative to the sisters of heterosexual men, thus compensating for any loss to the gene pool from gay men. This suggests that there is indeed a gay gene (or genes) conferring some type of reproductive advantage in the female relatives of gay men. Some researchers have speculated that it may be a "man-loving" gene, which, when found in men, makes them gay, but which, when found in women, makes them particularly likely to be attracted to (and thus form heterosexual relationships with) men, leading to lots of offspring and hence lots of gay (or "man-loving") genes. Even if there is a no "man-loving" gene making sisters reproduce more, a "gay" gene may still be of some advantage to an individual who carries this gene if it is associated with helping relatives' children survive and reproduce. So, for example, a gay man may help raise his sister's or brother's children, and thus his genes are replicated through helping kin, even if his genes aren't replicated sexually. Interestingly, there is some evidence for this mechanism in Samoan men with same-sex attraction, a group called the *Fa'afafine* (Vasey & VanderLaan, 2010). Samoan society is of some importance because it is likely closer than modern Western societies to the social and family relations that would have occurred when humans evolved.

As these examples attest, nature has myriad ways of creating and sustaining diversity, and what may seem like a genetic dead end, and thus biologically "unhealthy," may not be. So, that someone simply does not reproduce through a traditional heterosexual process does not mean that they are maladapted from an evolutionary perspective. It may just mean that there is another evolutionary mechanism at work beyond sexual reproduction that replicates the individual's genes.

There is also a broader point here: To say that something is adaptive is merely to say that it has evolutionary consequences in favor of gene replication. It is a description of a natural process of change over time. But as a description, should it bleed into moral reasoning? Evidence of an adaptation is not evidence of a moral (or even a "health") imperative. To think otherwise is in a certain sense to fall victim to the naturalistic fallacy, a reasoning error that assumes that what is natural must also be good or right. There are, of course, many examples of natural processes that most people would not consider to be at all good or right or healthy. HIV/AIDS and murder are two examples. But there is also no inherent moral superiority in one set of genes over another merely on the basis that one set replicates itself more frequently than another. They are merely chemicals, after all, whether they replicate themselves or not.

The brain might deceive us into thinking there is some inherent "rightness" in the replication of our genes. If so, however, this is a con job. Our genes create brain structures that give us emotions and tendencies that in turn tell us that certain things are more right than others. But is this so? Can we truly have an "objective" sense of rightness and wrongness related to reproduction that is independent of the whisperings of our genes?

We can also frame moral and health questions in different ways to show that their relevance and their answers are specific to context, time, and culture. For example, in modern society, one might pose this moral and health question: *Is it right and healthy to add more humans to a planet already suffering from overpopulation?* I imagine that this question would not have been posed, say, one hundred years ago, or, if it were, it probably would have prompted a different answer. In short, is there any ultimate truth, significance, or rightness to the replication of human DNA?

To summarize, an evolutionary perspective does not necessarily imply that asexuality is a disorder. But would asexuality be considered "pathological" from any other perspectives? Let's consider a number of these other perspectives (Bogaert, 2006b).

First, should asexual people be considered disordered and/or abnormal because they constitute a small minority and thus are statistically rare in the population? After all, to be *abnormal* is to deviate from the norm. If you think about it, I expect you will see that this is a poor criterion for pathology, because being a statistical rarity can be easily construed as positive and life enhancing in certain domains (e.g., exceptional musical talent, as mentioned earlier).

In modern medicine and psychology, individuals are not typically diagnosed with a (mental) pathology or dysfunction unless they experience "marked distress or interpersonal difficulty" (*DSM-IV-TR*) (American Psychiatric Association, 2000, p. 539).[2] For example, the most common type of disorder that asexual people may be diagnosed with is hypoactive sexual desire disorder, which is characterized by a marked lack of desire for sex, accompanied by, as mentioned, distress or interpersonal difficulty.

Currently, we have only a modest amount of data on the mental health of asexual people, so definitive conclusions about distress or other psychological disturbance issues in this group await future research. However, the research to date does not suggest that asexual people, as a whole, are distressed by their lack of sexual interest. Psychologists Nicole Prause and Cynthia Graham, and Lori Brotto and colleagues, found no evidence that self-identified asexuals were distressed by their asexuality (Prause & Graham, 2007; Brotto, Knudson, Inskip, Rhodes, & Erskine, 2010). For example, one participant in the Prause and Graham (2007) study reported, "I'm not worried about it or I'm not concerned about it. . . . My life is interesting enough and it's not really, um, a necessity" (p. 346).

Related research suggests that a high percentage of people (as many as 40 percent) in the United States report being very or extremely happy even if they have not had sex in the last year (Laumann, Gagnon, Michael, & Michaels, 1994). Of course, many of these people would not define themselves as asexuals or be defined as asexual using a common definition (i.e., enduring lack of sexual attraction). However, these results do indicate that a lack of sexuality, at least broadly defined, is not necessarily a reliable indicator of mental health or happiness. In addition, even if new research finds that some asexual people do have, on average, elevated rates of distress or other mental health issues, what would this actually mean? Well, let's consider some related research on other sexual minorities.

Elevated distress and mental health issues have been found in some gays and lesbians (Meyer, 2003). Does this mean that being gay or lesbian is a disorder? No. There is, for example, other evidence that many gays and lesbians are also happy, content, and free from serious mental health issues (Busseri, Willoughby, Chalmers, & Bogaert, 2006; Diamond, 2003a). Moreover, from a modern medical or psychological perspective (e.g., in the *DSM*), homosexuality is not viewed as pathological. So, even if some gays and lesbians do have an elevated level of distress or other mental health issues, this fact should not be used to pathologize all gays and lesbians or homosexuality in general. Similarly, if future research shows that asexual people do have an elevated level of distress or other mental health issue, this fact should not be used to pathologize all asexuals or asexuality in general.

Another important issue to consider is the *source* of the distress. Should we pathologize someone for feeling distressed because they do not fit in with the larger group or because the majority of people do not like them? Or, alternatively, should we pathologize the society itself for not tolerating minorities and diversity? In sum, there are several arguments against using *distress* (e.g., lack of evidence of increased distress, questions about the source of any distress that does exist) as a basis for pathologizing asexuality.

The second criterion often used to diagnose a mental disorder is interpersonal difficulty. Thus, should we consider asexual people disordered because they lack an important interpersonal dimension—sexuality? Again, not necessarily. Interpersonal relations do not *only* include sex. There are many aspects of social relations beyond sexuality, in which asexual people may function normally; that is, similarly to the majority of other people. Indeed, a sexual dysfunction is only diagnosed in modern medicine and psychology (e.g., in the *DSM*) if it has an effect on interpersonal relations *beyond* the specific sexual domain that is of issue. So, for asexual people, a lack of sexual interest is not per se a criterion for having a disorder, unless it causes other interpersonal issues. And, of course, celibates (e.g., nuns), by choice, never have sex with others and are not considered to have a pathology by modern medicine and psychology. Similarly, it does not make sense to pathologize asexual people, who by their natures lack sexual interest and attraction, for not engaging in sex with others.

But how about other (nonsexual) aspects of interpersonal relations— do asexual people have a broad level of interpersonal impairment beyond sexuality?[3] There is evidence that some asexual people may have an elevated level of atypical interpersonal functioning, such as increased social withdrawal (Brotto et al., 2010), but even if additional research bears this out, this, again, does not necessarily mean that we should pathologize *all* asexual people or asexuality in general.

An additional consideration is this: If an atypical biological process or physical health condition underlies asexuality, does this mean that asexuality is a disorder? For example, there is some evidence that health issues and atypical prenatal development may underlie the development of asexuality in some people (Bogaert, 2004). This research is important when we consider the origins of asexuality (see chapter 13), but, for two reasons, it should not guide our thinking on whether asexuality is a disorder. First, it is unlikely that physical health issues and atypical prenatal development underlie all instances of asexuality (Bogaert, 2004). Thus, even if many asexual people do have health issues (and/or atypical prenatal development), we cannot use this evidence to conclude that *all* asexual people are disordered or that asexuality per se is pathological. Second, using atypical sexual development as an indicator of a current mental health problem is a dubious approach. If so, we should also pathologize gays and lesbians as having a (current) mental disorder, as atypical prenatal development probably underlies, at least to some degree, the development of same-sex attraction (LeVay, 2010). If so, perhaps we should diagnose individuals with great musical talent as having a disorder, for atypical prenatal development (e.g., exposure to high prenatal hormones) may predispose one to having this talent (Manning, 2002). It is important, then, not to confuse the cause of a human psychological variation with a determination of whether that variation is currently construable as a mental illness.

It is also notable that the historical record does not show consistent evidence of asexuality as pathology; indeed, the opposite may be the case. For example, a lack of sexuality has been not seen as a disorder throughout the much of the history of Western medicine (Sigusch, 1998). Even today, some religions and cultures would not pathologize an absence of sexuality; instead, a lack of sexuality (or at least abstinence) is often considered a virtue. Thus, an absence of sexuality has not been considered a disorder consistently across time or across current cultural contexts.

Another issue relates to stigmatization. When we label someone as having a disorder, we often stigmatize them, and stigmatization itself can be a source of distress and mental health concerns. After all, who would not be stressed by being labeled "disordered"? The impact of stigmatization has been raised in the context of other sexual minorities (e.g., gays and lesbians) (Meyer, 2003). In short, why go down the road of labeling something as a disorder when there is evidence that it is not a disorder, and when we know that such labels themselves have negative consequences?

Aside from these arguments against pathologizing asexuality, there is lab research on arousal that may support the idea that asexuality is not a disorder. As mentioned in chapter 6, research has demonstrated that asexual women, like sexual women, show non-category-specific responding to sexual stimuli; that is, asexual women show some level of genital arousal to both male- and female-oriented sexual stimuli, very similar to heterosexual women and lesbians (Brotto & Yule, 2011). Thus asexual women do not show low arousal (i.e., abnormally low vaginal responses) to sexual activity, as women diagnosed as "dysfunctional" often do.[4] Indeed, the authors of the study argue that this work gives additional support to the idea that asexuality is a sexual orientation, like being gay or straight, because asexual women respond physically in ways that are very similar to their (non-dysfunctional) homosexual and heterosexual counterparts.

Let's return to the issue of distress, but from the flip side. There are often hidden benefits to asexuality that need to be considered when making a final determination about the question of whether asexuality is a sexual "disorder." In fact, psychologists Nicole Prause and Cynthia Graham found that asexuals report significant advantages to their asexuality. The top four were as follows: (1) avoiding the common problems of intimate relationships, (2) decreasing risks to physical health or unwanted pregnancy, (3) experiencing less social pressure to find suitable partners, and (4) having more free time (Prause & Graham, 2007, p. 351). Perhaps we can add to these the issue raised in chapter 8: Asexuality avoids the *madness of sex*. Let's call these point the big five benefits of asexuality.

At this point, you may be thinking: *Yes, the author is right that these arguments show that asexuality is not necessarily a disorder.* And yet, if you are a sexual person, you may also have a vague notion, a feeling you can't shake, that regardless of these arguments, asexual people still *must be missing something.* After all, doesn't (partnered) sex entail a special passion, excitement, and thrill, which asexuals must be missing out on?

Maybe. But who am I to say—and who are you to say—what passion is right for a given individual? Have you ever skydived before? Of course, most people haven't and have no interest in it. I have, and for me, it was a thrill. But do those who have not had, and do not want to have, this experience have a disorder? So, if you don't want this experience, should we diagnose you with, say, *hypoactive skydiving disorder* because you eschew this thrilling life activity?

I was recently invited to give a talk on asexuality to the Society for Sex Therapy and Research, or SSTAR. (Such organizations often try to find a catchy acronym to make their group memorable. I like theirs: "STAR" with a stutter.) SSTAR is the main conference for the world's sex therapists. Attendees come from a variety of backgrounds, including medicine, psychology, and social work, and all are trained (or in training) to help people with sexual problems.

Frankly, I was nervous to give a talk to SSTAR. Although trained in sexology, I'm an academic, and like most academics, my work primarily relates to teaching and research. Thus, unlike SSTAR members, I am not a sex therapist or even a clinician. These folks work in the trenches, even if those trenches sometimes lie on (or near) Madison Avenue and can be mined for gold. Thus, I did not know if I was a lone sheep set loose among two hundred battle-ready and hungry (clinical) wolves.

Another reason I was nervous was because a past surgeon general of the United States was in attendance. She was in one of the front rows looking at me, and I was looking at her.

However, the most important reason I felt nervous was because I was arguing that asexuality should not (necessarily) be construed as a disorder. Years before, I had gotten into fights—no, not fistfights—with some clinicians who I felt were putting inappropriate pressure on some asexuals to become sexual beings. Moreover, the majority of the attendees at SSTAR have spent their professional careers trying to increase (healthy) sexual behavior in their clients. Thus, I felt that they, like the few clinicians I had interacted with, would consider asexuality a disorder that needs fixing. So, my expectation was that I would be either coolly received or hotly dismissed.

In my talk—a bit shakily delivered, I have to admit—I unpacked many of the issues above, including various arguments against asexuality per se being viewed as a disorder, the contention that sex itself is a very odd activity that often causes mental lapses (see chapter 8 on the madness of sex), and the argument that, of course, passions differ among people. I also ended with the skydiving analogy mentioned above, complete with a picture of someone soaring through the air.

To my surprise (shock, in fact), there was hearty applause when I showed my skydiving picture and said my punch line: "If not interested in this activity, should you be diagnosed with *hypoactive skydiving disorder*?" Evidently, a significant number of clinicians, perhaps a majority of these modern therapists, recognized that sex is only one of many possible passions that people can have, and felt that we shouldn't impose our valued passions on others. In this applause, there may also have been recognition that some of their colleagues have possibly been overdiagnosing sexual problems and imposing, perhaps if only implicitly, their own values on others.

So, is there only one right way to live a human life?

NOTES

1. My language here (e.g., gay genes *compete*) is teleological; it suggests that genes have intentions, motives, or a purpose. Evolutionary types would be mad at me, as genes don't have these characteristics; that is, genes themselves don't "compete" for anything. So, to all you evolutionary types, please excuse my loose language, as I am using it in this way to help illustrate a point.

2. Note that the most important reference/source for understanding and diagnosing mental disorders in North America is the *Diagnostic and Statistical Manual of Mental Disorders* (*DSM*). Clinicians view it as their "bible."

3. This is assuming, of course, that we can agree on the definition of an interpersonal impairment.

4. Whether someone with low arousal should be construed as having a disorder (especially if he or she has no distress about it) is, of course, another issue to consider.

TEN

A Monster in All of Our Lives

John Money, perhaps the most famous twentieth-century sexologist after Alfred Kinsey, William Masters, and Virginia Johnson, was inspired once by a poem he read outside a cottage on Fire Island (an island retreat just outside of New York). The first line read, "There is a monster in all of our lives." Money amended the line, adding the adjective "unspeakable" to the word "monster," and used it to frame the main idea of one of his many books on sexology (Money, 1994). He believed that this phrase—*unspeakable monster*—was an apt description of the sexual and other secrets that often plague people. Thus, a monster is often lurking, although the person does not (or cannot) speak directly about it. However, an astute observer can discover it by some telltale signs, particularly irrational behaviors, as the person tries to cope with life's challenges.

There is a famous painting by seventeenth-century artist Henry Fuseli called *The Nightmare*, in which a sleeping woman is seductively draped over her bed, and a monster—in this particular case, an incubus—sits on her belly. An incubus is a legendary demonic creature that has intercourse with sleeping women. From a psychological perspective, the male incubus and its female equivalent (succubus) are creations of the mind that symbolize humans' powerful and uncontrollable sexual nature, along with, perhaps, our desire to abdicate to supernatural forces our personal responsibility for any disturbing sexual inclinations; hence, artful characters to represent Money's notion of an unspeakable monster.

Unspeakable monsters are specific to the time and the culture in which one grows up and lives; thus, they are partially socially con-

115

structed. Average adolescent boys from a strict Catholic upbringing in the 1950s in the Western world probably had masturbation as their unspeakable monster, whereas the masturbation monster of today for average adolescent American boys, Catholic and otherwise, may be less ferocious than it once was.

It is probably true that, if you accept Money's description, many sexual people have unspeakable (sexual) monsters. The chapter on the madness of sex attests to this fact: untold numbers of people have sexual secrets that plague them. But do some asexual people also have monsters, unspeakable and otherwise? Although not attracted to others in a traditional sense, asexual people may be sexual in other ways, and some may be reluctant to reveal this (Bogaert, 2008). For example, some asexual people may have odd paraphilias that they do not want to discuss with the world, and that perhaps they are even reluctant to admit to themselves. So, are some asexual people truly and utterly mad, just like the rest of the sexual planet?

At one point in my first paper on asexuality (Bogaert, 2004), I posed the following question: "How might people with atypical sexual proclivities respond to the statement, *I have never felt sexually attracted to anyone at all*?" This led me to ask whether some asexual people might have unusual sexual interests (i.e., paraphilias). After all, if someone is not attracted to people, they still might be attracted to something else. In a number of papers (Bogaert, 2004; Bogaert, 2006b; Bogaert, 2008), I suggested that this is an interesting possibility, but I also suggested that it is unlikely that a majority of asexual people have paraphilias, because "never having felt sexual attraction to anyone at all" implies no level of *human* partner involvement/interest. In short, it would exclude people who are gay, bisexual, or straight, as well as most people with an unusual sexual attraction (e.g., fetishists). This is because some level of sexual attraction to human beings remains within those with paraphilias, even if their primary interest is in a paraphilic object—for example, a fetishist's interest in women's high-heeled shoes. I also suggested that it is unlikely that most asexual people have an extreme paraphilia, because, first, they are quite rare, and second, most asexual people are women. Women are much less likely than men to have a paraphilia (Cantor, Blanchard, & Barbaree, 2009).

So, no (secret) sexual attractions in asexuals? Well, not necessarily. My contact with self-identified asexuals has suggested that some do indeed have very unusual sexual attractions, even if they have reported little or no sexual attraction to human beings (Bogaert, 2008). For example, some masturbating asexuals have indicated to me that there is a persistent theme, often very unusual, in their sexual fantasies. In other words, some people who lack attraction to others, some of whom identify as asexuals, do indeed have a paraphilia.[1]

Also, the issue raised in chapter 5 of the "disconnect" between fantasy and masturbation for some asexuals is relevant here. In particular, the fantasies of asexual people, when they do occur in a consistent or systematic way, often are constructed in such a way that they *themselves* are not part of the sexual acts they are fantasizing about or viewing (e.g., as in viewing a porn film)—in other words, they are not connected to anything or anyone sexual. It is as if their bodies, or (more correctly) aspects of their mind related to sexual arousal but not fully connected to their identity, need sexual stimulation to receive sexual release/pleasure. This is true even if their own identities, or who they are as individuals, are not sexual (i.e., not sexually attracted to others).

One asexual person on the AVEN website describes it this way: "I almost invariably think of fictional characters. My thoughts have never involved people I know, and they have never involved myself" (Vicious Trollop, 2005, July 25). Another on AVEN writes, "It's scenes in 3rd person; I may have a generic male character which is kind of me, but it's still separate from me, mentally watched rather than participated in" (Teddy Miller, 2005, July 25).

Still another AVEN participant writes, "The point isn't voyeurism, either: the scene doesn't turn me on because I'm watching it, it turns me on because it's sexually charged (and I'm acting as an emotional leech). I may have a character that I identify more with . . . but it's not a stand-in for me; it acts like a viewpoint character in fiction" (Eta Carinae, 2005, July 25).

These quotes suggest that some asexual people's fantasies, when they do have them, do not involve their own identities. Instead, their fantasies more often involve people they do not know or, more specifically, fictional characters or no one that could be connected to their identity in real life. These themes reinforce the idea that many masturbating asexuals may need sexual stimulation to receive sexual release/pleasure, but this stimulation is disconnected from their identities.

One question that emerges is this: Do these people have a "sexual orientation"—that is, a persistent erotic inclination toward others—given that they seek out and respond to consistent forms of sexual stimuli that contain people? This is an interesting question, at least to me. It might be argued that their bodies (or, more accurately, aspects of their brains related to arousal) do have a "sexual orientation" of sorts, but that they themselves, or their identities, do not.

A related question is whether these people are still truly "asexual," using a common definition of asexuals: a lack of sexual attraction (Bogaert, 2006b; Bogaert, 2008). After all, they are responding sexually, at least on a bodily level, to sexual content in their fantasies or in pornography; hence, a part of them must be sexually attracted to something if they are seeking out and responding to a specific sexual stimulus, rather than responding, say, to nothing at all or randomly.[2] Thus, on some level, sexual attraction occurs to something, including to others (e.g., in pornography or to/as fictional characters).

Even so, my answer is "yes," they are still asexual, at least in one sense: they have an absence of *subjective* sexual attraction. Subjective refers to the *I* or *me* in one's identity as a person, and if the person's *I* or *me* is not connected to something sexual, then they are asexual; they lack subjective attraction (Bogaert, 2006b). They—as individuals—are disconnected from their sexual responses to others or to sexual stimulation. In other words, they don't "own" those sexual attractions. Their bodies (or aspects of their brain regulating arousal) are responding to sexual stimulation on some level. The missing piece for them is the *I* or *me*, or an identity as an individual, in subjective sexual attraction. In other words, the *I* is missing in the statement "I am attracted to . . ."

A similar phenomenon may occur in some forms of transgenderism. A transgendered person who was born as a biological male, for example, may not "own" his masculine responses. This individual may behave in a traditional masculine way, he may appear masculine, and his body may respond to stimulation in a traditionally *masculine* way, even sexually. But if this person does not "own" her responses, and in fact is completely disconnected from them because of an internal sense of self as female, these masculine responses are not part of her identity, or her *I* or *me*.

Similar forms of disconnected sexuality have been discussed in the clinical literature on paraphilias. Indeed, this phenomenon may be construed as a rather exotic paraphilia, which literally means "beyond love," or "love beyond the usual." Thus, a paraphilia can mean that an individual has a sexual attraction to something unusual. It could also imply something broader: any kind of unusual sexual phenomenon associated with a person, and not merely a sexual attraction to something unusual. As a consequence, if you are keeping score, the label of "asexuality" could still apply to masturbating asexuals with "disconnected" fantasies, because their paraphilia is an unusual sexual phenomenon: there is no subjective sexual attraction to anything. Complicated indeed!

But back to the clinical literature on paraphilias: Ray Blanchard (1991) argues that some of these unusual sexual phenomena reflect alterations in the typical "targeting" process in human sexual attraction and sexuality in general. Our sexual attractions might occur when we connect our sexual feelings to others, as when we see or fantasize about someone, or perhaps our attractions are more responsive in nature, occurring when another person sees us and that incites or engages our sexual attractions to him or her. This "responsive" targeting system includes receptivity and object-of-desire mechanisms, and is more likely to occur in women (see also chapter 6 on gender). Both the more male-oriented and female-oriented target processes may ultimately relate to basic "mate-recognition" mechanisms (Bakker, 2003). In other words, these target processes are part of a larger mate-recognition system that humans use to seek out and choose reproductive partners.

But what if an individual's targeting system does not operate in this way? What if, for example, the "I" in "*I* am attracted to him or her" in a typical targeting sequence does not operate in a traditional way? In some asexual people, the disconnect between identity/self (the "I") and a sexual object seems to be this kind of target alteration: the identity or self is not connected to or "targeted" to a sexual object.

I am not aware of a specific name for this paraphilia. However, using a traditional Greek nomenclature, I have named it *autochorissexualism*: the quality of having sex without (*choris*) one's self/identity (*auto*), or "identity-less" sexuality (see also Bogaert, in press-b).

People without sexual attraction to others may also have other target-oriented paraphilias. For example, my experience is that some self-identified asexual people may have *automonosexualism*, in which the person is attracted to him- or herself sexually (Rohleder, 1907).[3] Blanchard argues that these paraphilias also reflect directional/target issues because, instead of directing one's sexual interests outward, one targets his or her sexual interests inward. Automonosexualism is rare and has sometimes been associated with transgendered individuals (Hirschfeld, 1948; Blanchard, 1991; Blanchard, 1989; Freund & Blanchard, 1993). For example, the phenomenon of autogynephilia (in which a man is sexually attracted to himself, but as a woman) is a type of automonosexualism (Blanchard, 1989; Lawrence, 2011).

But aren't these paraphilias—specifically, *autochorissexualism* and *automonosexualism*—disorders? So, one might agree that asexuality per se is not a disorder (see chapter 9), but surely these exotic paraphilias imply a disorder? Perhaps, but paraphilias are tricky mental health issues. Sexologists Charles Moser and Peggy Kleinplatz (2005), for example, have argued that paraphilias, or at least the original definition of them (as unusual sexual phenomena), should not necessarily be construed as disorders, partly because there is murkiness as to what construes a healthy sexuality in the first place. I agree. In fact, one might be so bold as to turn this issue on its head, expanding the definition of disorder to include not just atypical sexual fare but also sex in general, as it all may be construed as a form of madness (see also chapter 8).

To test more formally some of these ideas on autochorissexualism and automonosexualism, more research needs to be done on the sexual fantasies of masturbating asexuals. Some interesting studies examining the arousal responses of asexuals in the laboratory to various images, with narrations of the individual as a fictional character, and/or with images of the individual himself or herself (to assess for automonosexualism), could be conducted. In this way, we could find out more about any sexual proclivities, even secret ones, in asexual people.

Speaking of secrets, let's end with a bit more discussion on this issue: Are there any secrets left? Modern technology and communications have created the potential to expose one's inner life to probing and wide dissemination. Hence, even if one is highly motivated to keep one's life private, this may be hard to do, or at least harder to do than it once was, especially if the details of that private life are juicy. This is particularly true for sex, and other people's motivation to expose sexual details, especially if they are embarrassing or run counter to one's public profession, is often as strong as the individual's motivation to keep these details a secret. Even if others' motivation is not as strong as one's own motivation to maintain a private life, it is notable that we, as single individuals, are outnumbered by the throng, and thus there are lots of chances of exposure by one of the many people in the throng. The Internet, and Facebook in particular, are good examples of how quickly secrets are revealed in the modern world.

Interestingly, sex still makes good content as a juicy secret, but I expect that it is not as juicy as it once was. I think this is in part because modern communication has exposed so many "private" lives; thus, few sexual secrets shock anymore. Indeed, it is part of postmodern culture to be jaded and unfazed by sexual secrets. Sex is less of a big deal, and not to be hidden away in the same way as it used to be. So, it is still a monster, but one with less ferocity.

Why am I telling you all this? And what does it have to do with asexuality? Because the two points I have made here—there are no more secrets, and sexuality is less of a taboo to keep hidden than it once was— are both relevant to the issues of paraphilias and asexuality. First, people are less motivated to keep their sexual lives, or the lack thereof, hidden. So, do I believe people when they tell me that they are asexual? Well, yes, even if it is a bit of a qualified "yes." Moreover, self-identified asexuals may not hide unusual sexual interests, if they do have them. Second, if people have a secret sex life (e.g., a paraphilia that they don't want to reveal), this can still be found out. With their secrets revealed, these people will join the throng of others displaying sexual monsters on their backs, even if these monsters are less ferocious and less unspeakable than they once were.

NOTES

1. It is important to remember that many asexuals do not masturbate and/or have no fantasies (or at least no consistent theme in them), and hence do not have a paraphilia (see chapter 5 on masturbation).

2. Although I think this discussion on paraphilias is important, it must always be remembered that some masturbating asexuals do not direct their sexual responses to anything, or they direct their masturbation to situations or objects in a more or less random way, and still others do not masturbate at all (see more in chapter 5 on masturbation).

3. Automonosexualism might still retain the characteristic of a lack of sexual attraction to others, but, technically, there would still be a sexual attraction to someone, even if it were only to oneself. Thus, automonosexualism is not a case of asexuality using the strict definition of "lacking a subjective sexual attraction."

ELEVEN

Art and Food on Planet Sex

In chapter 8, I introduced an old man who said that, nowadays, the bathing beauties in the famous *Sports Illustrated* swimsuit issue "did nothing" for him. I suggested that his newfound sexless world had something in common with a lifelong asexual person's world. I also suggested that average sexual people may also have glimpses of this world when their normally sexed brains are turned off for brief periods.

Though sexual people may have temporary glimpses of what asexual people experience, this is not to say that sexual people's brushes with sexual disinterest capture perfectly the true "phenomenology" of the asexuality. Recall that asexual people are likely a diverse bunch, so one type of lens on the world of sexuality (or asexuality) does not fit all. In addition, for many asexual people, an even deeper level of disconnection to the sexual world occurs than what is suggested by, for example, the old man's current take on sex, or other sexual people's bouts of sexual disinterest. This is because many asexual people have a complete (or nearly complete) lack of sexual attraction, not just a lack of current sexual interest. Thus, returning to our example of the old man, he did recognize that these swimsuit models were sexually attractive. Perhaps he could have mustered some level of sexual interest if one of these bathing beauties magically appeared in his apartment, ready for some action. Or perhaps he would have been titillated by these images if he were given a booster shot of testosterone, as there is evidence that this hormone is linked to sex drive and declines with age (Lamberts, van den Beld, & van der Lely, 1997).

For many asexual people, such inducements (e.g., swimsuit models appearing fantasy-like in one's bedroom; a shot of testosterone) would likely have little effect. For many asexual people, there is likely no *underlying* sexual attraction at all; that is, there is no sexual connection that can be pulled to the surface, and perhaps even no real recognition that these models are "sexually attractive," except perhaps on an abstract level, having taken in our culture's norms and standards of sexual beauty. Thus, asexual people probably experience the sexual world, inducements notwithstanding, differently than the rest of the planet.

In this chapter, I explore the phenomenology (or lived experience) of asexuality; more specifically, this chapter is an exploration of a *hypothetical* lived experience, as I ask what life would be like if all people were asexual. I do this to give insight into the lives of asexual people, but also to see how embedded sex is within many human cultures, both past and present. So, what would a sexless planet (or, more specifically, a sexless culture) truly be like? To answer this question, let us speed by the glaringly and often numbingly obvious aspects of our oversexed pop culture—including pornography, TV shows' titillation, or, yes, the swimsuit edition of *Sports Illustrated*—and head into the subtle and deeper recesses of our sex-infused culture. Thus, let's touch on those areas of our culture that seem immune to its influence, yet may not be. To begin, let's venture into one of the more refined areas of our culture on Planet Sex: art.

I have no talent for it, but I have a fondness for fine art, especially painting. My interest derives partly from exposure to painting through some of my family and friends, some of whom do in fact have a talent for it. While wandering through galleries, eyeing renderings from various classical and modern eras, it is hard to avoid the conclusion that sexual interest and attraction has always driven, at least partly, aesthetic sensibilities. The nude in particular—especially the female nude—has been standard content for years, and it is difficult not to conclude that the sexuality of the primarily male, heterosexual artists who created these images, in both Western and non-Western societies, has had a major impact on these works.

Indeed, I sometimes wonder as I stroll around galleries what the history of art would be like without sex—broadly defined—as a subject matter. This extends into subject matters and content in art beyond the depictions of (female) nudes, although I am using this example to illustrate my point. I've even imagined, with tongue in cheek, whether curators might close down their galleries if for some reason a woman's body was not allowed to be shown, as there would be no be art left to display! I've imagined big, flashing neon signs outside of galleries announcing, *Gallery closed due to shortage of nudes. . . . Gallery closed due to shortage of nudes. . . . Gallery closed due to shortage of nudes. . . .*

Of course I am exaggerating the point, as there is a myriad of themes in art beyond women's bodies. I am also not arguing that nudity and the human body are found in art only because of people's sexual attraction to them. After all, nudity and the human body itself have been portrayed in art to illustrate various "nonsexual" themes—for example, the creation story in Albrecht Dürer's *Adam and Eve* could be construed as such. Indeed, there is a tradition in art of distinguishing "the nude" from "the naked." "The nude" shows the unclothed body because it is integral to or part of the natural condition of the subject or the scene (e.g., Greek gods were often depicted without clothes) (Clark, 1956). In contrast, with "the naked," a sexual intent is often presumed if the unclothed state is not a natural condition of the subject or the scene (e.g., a nurse still wearing part of her uniform).

Yet there is ambiguity here, as the meaning of "natural" is dubious, as is the distinction between nudity and nakedness. Isn't being out of one's clothes, even partially, more *natural* than, say, wearing a uniform? Art critic Charles Darwent (2008) also points out that the distinction between nude and naked is often blurred and slippery. He uses a painting by Philip Wilson Steer called *Seated Nude: The Black Hat* to illustrate his point. In this painting, an attractive woman is seated without clothes, but she does have on her head an elaborate black hat. Steer evidently never allowed this painting to be viewed. He was influenced by some of his friends, who argued that the woman's "nudity" (and of course the title indicates that this is a "nude") was in fact an instance of "nakedness," in part because the affectation on her head implies, presumably, an unnatural and sexualized context.

One might also argue that the "nude" body, even when not portrayed to illustrate directly sexual themes, is affected, at least indirectly, by the artist's sexuality and/or sexual elements that are embedded in his or her culture. For example, are the nudity and temptation themes in the creation story of Adam and Eve truly without sexual connections? Of course not: this biblical creation story is itself, partially, about sex. Thus, Dürer's sexual attractions likely inspired him, if only on an unconscious level, to create a painting that included these themes. In other words, this story was, arguably, aesthetically interesting and pleasing to him because of his sexual attractions. That members of the public (or the patrons who commissioned this work) also wanted and/or were drawn to such portrayals also speaks to the power of sexuality in the production of this and related art. Note, too, that the two main figures—Adam and Eve—in this famous painting have fig leaves covering their genitals. This depiction is true to the events in the biblical creation story itself, as both Adam and Eve covered themselves with fig leaves after eating from the tree of knowledge. However, sexual mores probably influenced why this portion of the creation story—and not the innocent, completely nude period of this story—was depicted in this and in so many other versions of it. For example, it can be argued that Dürer was affected by his and society's (e.g., the Catholic Church's) view that public nudity was shameful, or at least sexually immodest, not just in reality but also in artistic depictions. This social construction of sex as "shameful" also derives from the power of sexual attractions, along with a (neurotic) desire to control them.

You may be thinking that the female nude in art and popular culture must only have a special resonance, aesthetic and otherwise, for heterosexual men (i.e., male artists and male patrons), and thus heterosexual women wandering the great galleries must have a disconnected experience, similar perhaps to the non sequitur experienced by average asexual people. After all, shouldn't the portrayal of only *men's* bodies have a special resonance, aesthetic and otherwise, for heterosexual women? I think this is partially true, but a straightforward conclusion of this kind does not capture some of the subtlety and complexity of female sexuality. As mentioned in chapter 6 on gender, women's sexuality is also affected by "object-of-desire" concerns, and there may be a strong aesthetic appreciation of the female body as an object of desire, sexually and romantically, in the eyes of men (Bogaert & Brotto, in progress; Bogaert, Visser, Pozzebon, & Wanless, 2011). Thus, heterosexual women's sexual interests, attractions, and desires at times may still resonate, perhaps very strongly, with the depiction of the female nude form. That many heterosexual women are strongly interested in viewing beautiful women in fashion forums (e.g., fashion magazines) and in the general media (e.g., on TV, on the Internet) supports this view (Bogaert & Brotto, in progress).

Some of these points are arguable, perhaps, but what is likely not arguable is that our cultural products are strongly influenced in ways beyond our realization by human sexual attractions and how these play themselves out in the society in which the artist lives. If so—to return to our original question—what would our art galleries be like if all the artists were completely asexual? Before I answer this question, however, let me address a caveat: There may exist now or in the past asexual artists who, in their art, give commentary on being asexual in a sexual world. Thus, asexual people might still produce "sexual" art as a form of social or personal commentary. But I am more curious about what kind of art asexual artists would produce if they ruled the art world and their asexual brethren ruled the rest of the world. In other words, what would it be like if art had no aesthetic linkage to sexuality whatsoever?[1] Would depicting a nude (and the genitals in particular) have the same fascination, and garner the same attention, as depicting, say, the middle toe does for sexual artists? I expect that in a completely asexual world, art would be very different indeed. Thus, the current bevy of nude paintings—even those that on the surface seem not to have a sexual connection, but undoubtedly do, such as Dürer's *Adam and Eve*—would turn into a scattered few. Moreover, all of this to-do about what is "nude" and what is "naked" deeply reflects our sexual natures, along with our personal and cultural neuroticism about them. Thus, if we were all truly asexual, such distinctions would not arise in the first place; they would be nonissues.

My analysis here suggests that culture (or at least the meanings we derive from it) is not randomly generated but instead reflects, at least partly, our basic wishes, desires, and preferences—in short, our individual and our collective human natures. And, of course, for most people, that nature *is* sexual. Humans are also very visual animals, and thus it is not surprising that our sexualized pop culture and art reflects this visual acuity and fascination. So human art is particularly likely to be a *visual* reflection of our basic wishes, desires, and preferences, including our sexual ones. If dogs ruled the world—and, of course, some dog owners believe that this is already so—then there might be equally elaborate *smell*-oriented pop culture and art that reflected canines' basics wishes, desires, and preferences, including sexual ones. Of course, the idea that culture partially maps onto human nature is not new, as there are many theories of culture that include as a tenet that human inclinations create, select, and give meaning to cultural products.[2]

Would an asexual person's presumed lack of sexual aesthetics extend to a lack of appreciation for all aspects of beauty in the human form? I noted in chapter 3 (on history) that one asexual man, the famous mathematician Paul Erdos, was preoccupied, including aesthetically, by mathematics: "If numbers aren't beautiful, I don't know what is" (Schechter, 1998, p. 7).

Yet there is complexity here. Some asexual people may have an appreciation of faces and the body on an abstract level, having taken in our culture's norms and standards of beauty. In addition, some asexual people may still have a deep recognition and lure for "romantic" beauty in others of their preferred sex if they are romantically inclined. Third, humans may have an innate recognition of beauty, independent of both romantic and sexual attraction to others. Indeed, innate "beauty" and "ugliness" sensors may exist in the human brain, and this may have to do with tendencies to approach or avoid others in the evolutionary past. For example, our ancestors may have avoided unattractive people because their unappealing features could have been a sign of a potentially contagious disease processes, and thus they would have been important to avoid. Interestingly, research has shown that infants prefer to gaze at beautiful faces more than average or unattractive faces (Langlois, Roggman, Casey, & Ritter, 1987). Thus, the mind's beauty-recognition mechanisms may be partially decoupled from the mechanisms associated with both romantic and sexual attraction, and an asexual person may still retain some level of this appreciation for beauty.

Here is a quote suggesting that an aesthetic appreciation of others can occur in asexual people: "I could be attracted to someone. I can . . . you know, think they're good looking and think they're interesting and want to spend time with them and get to know them better. But to me it's never, oh, yeah, I hope we end up in bed" (Brotto, Knudson, Inskip, Rhodes, & Erskine, 2010, p. 610).

Another asexual person felt similarly: "I love the human form and regard individuals as works of art . . . but I don't ever want to come into sexual contact with even the most beautiful of people" (Scherrer, 2008, p. 626).

That having been said, much of the nudity and sex in popular culture and art must be a "disconnect" for many asexual people. A woman I know, when confronting the fact that she does not conform to many aspects of a traditional feminine gender role, utters the phrase, "I must have missed that day at girl school . . ." Painterly-minded asexual people wandering around galleries with a bevy of nudes at eye level might simi-larly utter the phrase, "I must have missed that day at art school . . ."

I must admit that I have cheated in my discussion of art and sexuality. Art is a relatively easy subject matter to deconstruct from a sex point of view, and indeed, I have thought about the sex/art connection for a num-ber of years. As a more difficult challenge, I played a game—a kind of thought experiment—to see if I could find an aspect of modern life and culture untouched by human sexuality. One day at lunch over a bowl of soup, I thought I had, true to my task, thrown myself a curveball and succeeded. I said out loud, "Aha, *food!*"

On the surface, it seems that the world of food and the world of sex are far removed from one another. They are related to different desires and thus, presumably, occupy very different "psychological spaces" in people's heads and exist in very different domains of our lifestyles and cultures.

However, I quickly realized that this was not true. It did not take long before the sexual connections to food started coming to mind—and I don't just mean "cheesy" ones, such as the Food Network sexing up its shows with an attractive chef/host or two (no, I don't mean replaying old episodes of Julia Child).

Here are the four sexual connections that came to mind relatively quickly: First, food intake and its control are major life concerns for many people—particularly young women—in their attempts to achieve a maxi-mally attractive body. Achieving an ideal or optimal object-of-desire level through a beautiful/sexy body allows a woman to have great advantages in choosing the man (or the men) with whom she mates. This is because men place a greater value on women's physical attractiveness than wom-en place on men's, so women's bodies are of greater value and demand a higher price in the sexual marketplace. But women are not necessarily trying to satisfy only their current partner (if they have one); they are also trying to satisfy an "ideal," which, from an evolutionary perspective, allows them much greater opportunities to mate successfully, even be-yond their current mate. The current ideals are often influenced by the images shown in modern media of (arguably distorted) extremely attrac-tive people, the likes of whom would have been rarely seen for most of our evolutionary history; however, they are readily seen now and have been taken on as modern "ideals" nevertheless. Unfortunately, these "ideals" are so high (and often so unrealistic) (Wolf, 1991) that they are unlikely to be met by the vast majority of women, even if women implicitly perceive them as a way to reproductive success. As a consequence, women are more prone to body dissatisfaction than men, and this is a relatively consistent trend across time (Cash, Morrow, Hrabosky, & Perry, 2004; Mazur, 1986). Women compare their bodies to these "ideal" object-of-desire forms, as represented by supermodels and movie stars, even if the images of bodies portrayed are unrealistically thin or beautiful. But the vast majority of women cannot live up to these ideals. They ultimately put pressure on many women to make themselves beautiful and sexy—to become an ideal object of desire (see also chapter 6 on gender). Controlling food intake—through dieting—is a method women use to live up to this ideal and be maximally attractive to potential mates.

Somewhat in contrast, consider a second food/sex connection: Freud and other psychodynamically minded theorists have argued that overeating can result from defensive processes, including *sublimation*, or channeling ungratified sexual energy into another activity (in this particular case, eating).[3] If this is true, one might wonder whether the current obesity epidemic is partly the result of such a process. Is there something about the modern Western world that is creating a slew of sexually unsatisfied humans channeling their hunger for sex into an appetite for potato chips and candy bars? I also have wondered whether the "middle-aged spread" of so many male suburbanites results from sublimation, when the harem-like pursuits of their teenage and twenty-something years are replaced by a thirty-something domestication: a less sexually stimulating, but more calming certainty of a one-woman marriage. However, one might argue that this reasoning is off base and that one should expect the exact opposite, as our sexual desires are presumably being met more in the modern Western world than they ever have been before (e.g., compare today with, say, the presumed innocence of the 1950s). Actually, I don't think so. I think—again, perhaps in line with a quasi-Freudian interpretation—that our sexual desires are being met less than they ever have been. This is in part because the modern Western media are raising our sexual expectations, which seems to suggest that hyper-sexed athletes are the societal norm. Thus, even though the reality of people's sex lives is staying the same, relative to our raised expectations, we are coming up short, sexually speaking.

Another food connection is this: Dietary practices are influenced by sex hormones. There is, for example, evidence that men and women differ in their taste preferences—men being more focused on meat and women being more focused on sweets and fats, a difference that occurs even in children (Caine-Bish & Scheule, 2009). This gender difference is related, at least indirectly, to sex hormones, because these hormones partly underlie sexual differentiation, the process whereby male and female fetuses differentiate before birth. There is also evidence that sex hormones play a role in women's salt preferences across the menstrual cycle (Curtis & Contreras, 2006). Similar differences have been found in other species (e.g., salt preference over the estrus cycle in female rats). One reason women, relative to men, may have more of a craving for sweets and fats is to build up fat for their curvy bodies. Relative to women, men may crave meat more because their bodies require more protein to build muscle mass.[4]

Here is one final food example: Humans have long searched for the perfect aphrodisiac to drive their lovers wild and to increase their sex drive/potency. In fact, countless animals have been slaughtered and others driven to near extinction so that humans could extract and then ingest their body parts in the name of better sex. The Chinese seem especially susceptible to the (often misguided) notion that sexual powers reside in food, sometimes with dire ecological consequences. For example, the Chinese belief that the scales of the pangolin, or scaly anteater, have aphrodisiac qualities has led to the near extinction of this animal in Southeast Asia. Similarly, the Chinese belief in the aphrodisiac qualities of the rhino's horn, with its suggestive phallic shape and angle, has also been this animal's undoing, with it likewise being driven to near extinction. Of course, the fact that humans believe that sex and what we ingest are related, even if they are not (and thus foods have no true aphrodisiac qualities), is also testament to the fact that humans imbue nearly everything around us with special sexual meanings.

In short, it does not take long to find sexual connections to what seems like, on the surface at least, an aspect of our culture and lifestyle—food—that has no sexual relevance. For closure's sake, let's explore how these food examples might impact asexuality. In the first example, if dieting and related body-image issues are often driven by mating concerns, might asexual people never or rarely have dieting problems? Perhaps even a bolder prediction could be made: there may be no asexual bulimics (or at least no asexual people who have become bulimic). This is not to say that asexual women may not be concerned about their body image for reasons other than sex/mating (i.e., finding a romantic partner if ro-mantically inclined) but I expect their body-image issues and control of food consumption to differ from those of sexual women.

Let's return to the second example, and take, for the sake of argument, a skeptical view of asexuality, along with a Freudian bent. Some might argue that so-called asexual people are extremely repressed sexual peo-ple, and thus the level of sublimation in them should be even higher than in average sexual people. Hence, one might pose the following question, perhaps somewhat tongue-in-cheek: Should all asexual people be fat? However, if there is no "sexual" psyche to operate on in asexual people, then sublimation should not occur (i.e., overeating or any other defensive behaviors to deal with this bottled-up sexual energy; see chapter 12 on humor and sex). Thus, should they be thin, or at least not overeat? There are some interesting studies that suggest that sexual energy in repressed men, after being stimulated by an attractive woman, is defensively dis-charged (e.g., by unknowingly creating sexual double entendres or "Freudian slips"; see chapter 12 on humor). If so, there may be future research studies examining how asexual people respond to such sexual cues. Also, if one disregards the quasi-Freudian analysis altogether (and some would certainly think it is bunk!), perhaps one should expect asexu-als to become pleasantly plump, as their appetitive drives should be more focused on food (and not sex) in a culture that offers caloric abundance.

In the third example on taste preferences, should asexual people, if not only sexless but also somewhat genderless (see chapter 6), be im-mune to the influence of sexual hormones, not just in their sexual prefer-ences, but also indirectly in food preferences? There could be some inter-esting studies waiting in the wings related to menstrual cycle fluctuations in asexual women, and the degree to which their food preferences are affected by such fluctuations.

Is there any research on food-related behavior and/or weight in asexu-al people? Not much. In one study, I found that asexuals were slightly lighter than sexual people (Bogaert, 2004). Does this mean, then, that they are less inclined to "sublimate" with food, because there is no sexual energy to sublimate? Not necessarily. These were *average* differences, and so there was certainly a range of weights for asexual people in that study. Moreover, the asexual people were slightly shorter, so the decreased weight might have been partly a function of the slightly smaller stature of asexual people relative to sexual people (see more on this in chapter 13).

Third, in a follow-up study, I found no difference in weight between asexuals and sexual people (Bogaert, in press-a). Fourth, weight is, of course, a bit of a crude marker of food-related habits, some of which may still differ significantly between sexual and asexual people. Thus, more research needs to be conducted on food-related behaviors in asexual people. One thing is for sure, though, regarding eating habits and asexuality: Our planet would likely be a better place, ecologically speaking, if more people were asexual, because asexual people are not likely to hunt down animals to consume them for their real or imagined effect on increasing libido and potency.

SUMMARY

In this chapter, I attempted to reveal how deeply embedded sex is in our lifestyle and culture, and to argue that it should give us pause when we think sex is removed from our day-to-day activities and even our loftiest of cultural practices. For example, our aesthetic sense is undoubtedly affected by our attractions, and our sexual attractions are particularly potent ones when artists apply paint to canvas (or create work in any other medium). Even food and its consumption—the example I chose because I felt, at least initially, that it is immune to the powers of sex—are in reality often influenced by sexual issues. Finally, the analysis in this chapter may offer a glimpse into the sometimes alien and disconnected reality of an asexual person as he or she resides on Planet Sex.

NOTES

1. Of course, if we were an asexual species, our bodies would be radically different, particularly the genitals and secondary sex characteristics (see chapter 3). Thus the depiction of the nude human body in art would also necessarily be different. But indulge me here and assume that our bodies would be the same as they are now, as this exercise partly concerns how a sexual species with an elaborate culture, like ours, creates products infused with sex.

2. Therefore, my view would be similar to those of numerous (and even more biologically oriented) theorists who have written on the intermingling of biological tendencies and culture. These theorists often do not pull punches and are upfront about biology, or at least biological processes, taking the reins of the cultural horse, by offering such titles as *Genes, Mind and Culture: The Coevolutionary Process* (Lumsden & Wilson, 1981) and *Culture and the Evolutionary Process* (Boyd & Richerson, 1985). Richard Dawkins has also argued (e.g., in *The Selfish Gene*, 1976) that cultural ideas, like

genes, are "selected for" (like Darwin's natural selection) if they have a special reso-nance with people in a given time or place. He calls them "memes," and, yes, it is probably no coincidence that this word sort of rhymes with "genes." Note, however, that by suggesting a similarity between my view and these biologically oriented theo-ries of culture, I don't mean to imply that all of our wishes, desires, and preferences are fully biologically determined. They are not.

3.   There is some evidence that defensive processes can be involved with eating habits and disorders (Poikolainen, Kanerva, Marttunen, & Lönnqvist, 2001).

4.   Even if one agrees that taste preferences are influenced by "sex" hormones, does this mean that "sexuality" causes these food preferences? For example, one could argue that the true sexual connection here is indirect at best, because these sex hor-mones influence food preferences through their effect on biological sex/gender, and not through their impact on "sexuality" per se. Thus, am I conflating sexuality influ-ences with prenatal hormonal influences on biological sex and gender? Perhaps. As mentioned in chapter 6, however, sex and gender are so intertwined with sexuality, and vice versa, that to argue that only sex/gender (completely independently of sexu-ality) is a significant influence here is misleading. Also, given that these hormones vary across the menstrual cycle and evidently have an impact on food preferences, they are not just acting to cause "prenatal" sex/gender differences but also likely relate to day-to-day adult activities, including sexuality.

TWELVE

(A)sexuality and Humor

My aunt told me a joke or, as she called it, "a little story." A man is at the dentist with an impacted wisdom tooth. Needing oral surgery, the man is advised by the dentist that a Novocain injection is necessary. Unfortunately, for some reason, the injection does not seem to numb the man's mouth. So, the dentist advises another injection of Novocain. This second attempt at numbing the man's mouth also does not seem to work. Somewhat perplexed, the dentist next advises that a general anesthetic will be necessary to put the man under. However, even this approach is not effective, as the man remains awake and alert. A bit desperate now, the dentist reaches into the back of the medicine cabinet, and pulls out a bottle of blue pills.

The man asks, "So, what's that?"

"Viagra," the dentist answers.

The man exclaims, "Viagra! But why?"

"Well," the dentist replies, "because you're going to need *something* to hold on to when I pull that damn tooth!"

The content of humor is often sexual in nature. Why? It may partly have to do with our tendency to experience tension in relation to sexual matters, and this tension may serve as a readably accessible psychic "fuel" for driving the mechanics of laughter and humor. The philosopher/poet Herbert Spencer (1860) and the psychoanalyst Sigmund Freud (1960), along with more recent theorists (Zillmann & Bryant, 1980), have championed variations on "tension relief" models of humor, partly to help explain the sex/humor association, although these models can be applied to other tension-related content in humor too.

Sexual tension can come in two forms. First, there is what might be called a "natural" kind of sexual tension, as human sexual response is associated with a buildup of both physical arousal (e.g., vaginal lubrication, erections) and psychic arousal (feeling "turned on"). Yet even catching a glimpse of a hot-bodied passerby has the ability to arouse some titillating psychic tension. Thus sex is naturally associated with tension, both when actually engaging in it and when we are briefly reminded of it. Some sexual tension, however, is often more neurotic in nature. This is the kind of tension to which Freud and others largely referred. Neurotic sexual tension is created by most cultures in their tendency to limit and control sexual expression. Parents, teachers, lawmakers, police, and others are the primary agents of this control, as they act as socializers and enforcers of the rules and regulations of sex. In short, people have bottled-up neurotic sexual tension because they can't always do what they want sexually. This is a fact of civilized life, at least if you believe Freud and similarly minded scholars. Moreover, even the most sexually liberated among us cannot entirely escape these repressive clutches of the agents of civilized society, and thus even the most sexually liberated people still retain some residual neurotic sexual tension. Some people, though, have more pent-up neurotic sexual tension than others, perhaps because of their sensitive dispositions or perhaps because of a particularly rigid and repressive childhood.

This tension or "psychic energy"—natural or neurotic in origin—may be diverted and used as the fuel that helps drive laughter and humor. When the best comedians, amateur and professional alike, tell a joke or an amusing story, they provide rich detail and aptly time their punch lines, because these devices aid in building and releasing tension for full comic effect. Sex is an easy subject matter through which comedians ply their trade. This is in part because the tension necessary for full comic effect is already there; it just needs the right details and some good timing to harness and release it in the right way.

Laughter is pleasurable for most people, and part of the pleasure has to do with a release of tension. The release of tension, whichever way it is achieved, is pleasurable. Interestingly, the physical mechanisms of tension relief involved with laughter are similar to that of an orgasm—spasmodic muscle contractions (myotonia). Perhaps it is not surprising, then, that energy created in one domain—sexuality—may be harnessed and effectively released through another—laughter/humor—with similar physical mechanisms. Or at least that is the theory behind tension-reduction models of humor. Indeed, some theorists have speculated that one of the adaptive functions of laughter in humans, the only species that laughs,[1] is that it allows for the release of all kinds of psychic tension, which may be unhealthy if pent up too long. If we weren't able to laugh, so the theory goes, we would all eventually explode, at least psychically.[2]

A corollary of this type of tension-release theory of humor, at least of the classical Freudian version, is that once we laugh and tension is released, we should not only feel relieved but also have less of a need to release this energy in other ways, because the tension is, presumably, gone. Thus, a "catharsis" should occur, a temporary reduction of pent-up psychic energy and, importantly, a decreased tendency to engage in the tension-causing behavior. For example, if sex caused our tension, which has now been released in the form of a sexual joke, we should have a decreased need to have sex or a sexual outlet.

Is there modern scientific support for this tension-reduction model of humor, given that it is associated with some relatively ancient and oft-criticized theorists, such as Freud? There is, at least for some basic elements of the theory. Several relatively modern theorists of humor argue that some kind of tension is often important for and can enhance humor, particularly in humorous situations that evoke the act of laughter or other overtly mirthful reactions. For example, in a study by psychologists Dolf Zillmann and Jennings Bryant (1980), the authors found that when tension is high, people laugh and express more mirth. More specific to sexuality, though, there is also evidence that people who report a high degree of sexual desire (sexual tension) seem to enjoy sexual humor more than those who report lower sexual desire (Prerost, 1995).

But is there evidence that sexual tension can be *unconsciously* channeled into sexual humor, or what might be construed as "humor-like" behavior? The evidence here is indirect. Two studies in the 1980s suggested that sexual titillation makes men susceptible to creating inadvertent sexual puns or double entendres (Motley & Camden, 1985). In both of these studies, men thought they were in a fairly mundane "language and dialect" research experiment. This was a guise to hide the true goal of the studies: the investigation of Freudian humor-like behavior. In the first study, the researchers found that men more likely to complete sentences with sexual charged-meanings if they had a sexy female experimenter conduct the study than men who had a male (and thus presumably not so sexy) experimenter. For example, in the presence of a sexy female experimenter, men often completed the sentence "The lid won't stay on regardless of how much I" with the words *screw it*. This phrase has, of course, more sexual meaning than other ways of completing this sentence (e.g., *tighten it, turn it*). In a second, related study, the men who had the most "repressed" sexual personalities were the most likely to be susceptible to these types of inadvertent sexual puns. Presumably, the erotic tension created by the sexy female experimenter was unconsciously channeled into a subtle form of sexual expression and hence partially released in the form of these sexual puns and double entendres.

So, in short, sexual tension (whether recognized by the person or not) may relate to the production and appreciation of sexual humor.[3] But why is any of this—interesting though it may be—relevant to asexuality? It is relevant because sexual humor and the way it functions may reveal something about asexuality and vice versa; that is, asexuality may reveal how sexual humor functions. For example, are asexual people immune to sexual humor, because they, presumably, have so little sexual tension? Or, to put it in another way, do asexual people "get" sexual humor on a deep level, or on any level? And does this present a sneaky way of finding out whether asexual people are truly sexual (deep down)—to see if they laugh at a sexual joke? If they do laugh, does this not imply that there is some sexual energy/motive being discharged or released? *Got you! You laughed. You must be sexual!*

Did you laugh at the Viagra joke at the beginning of this chapter? (Or, if you had heard it before, did you laugh the first time you read it, or the first time someone told it to you?) Let's analyze the reasons why someone might or might not laugh at this joke. Of course, there are differences among people in how much they laugh in general, and so, of course, some of the individual differences in humor appreciation have to do with basic variations in personality and temperament (e.g., happiness, gregariousness, jolliness). But let's take this out of the equation for now, and concentrate on the account of humor appreciation and susceptibility put forward by Freud and company—namely, that it often has to do with the release of, or is at least facilitated by, sexual tension. Given the sexual content of this joke, a straightforward interpretation driven by this theory would say that those who have tension about their sexuality are more likely to laugh at this joke.

However, even if we accept the tension-reduction model of humor, we also need to realize that other elements are important for this joke to be effective. In particular, besides tension, a person also must *cognitively* "get" the joke. So, the individual must understand how the detail and the punch line create and then resolve (even in a bizarre way) the conflict posed by the story. Thus, in addition to an effective use and release of tension, the humorist must provide a satisfactory and meaningful resolution to the puzzle or situation raised in the joke. To accomplish this, the information in the joke or story must be relevant (i.e., "meaningful") on some level to the individual, or at least have some connection to activities that the individual is familiar with, so that he or she ultimately can "get" the joke.

Interestingly, the satisfactory resolution provided by the punch line (if a person does "get it") usually involves some kind of incongruity. In other words, it may involve holding two seemingly contradictory ideas together simultaneously, or some unexpected twist—thus, a bit of a surprise ending or a clever reversal of fortune. Yet this incongruity or twist usually still resolves the conflict or drama in some meaningful way, even if bizarrely so. And the person who appreciates this humor must get (on some level) that a resolution, incongruous as it may be, has occurred.

Incongruity forms the basis of a number of theories of humor. One modern theory of humor that incorporates incongruity as a main concept is the "benign violation" model (McGraw & Warren, 2010). In this view, for something to be funny, it must break a norm or a rule, but it must do so *benignly*. The incongruity lies in the fact that we must hold two contradictory ideas in mind simultaneously: first, that a norm is being violated (which is bad), but, second, that this violation is only a gentle or benign one (which is not so bad). There is a saying in comedy, attributed to the Irish novelist Kate O'Brien, that captures the essence of this theory: "If it bends, it's funny; if it breaks, it is not funny" (1-Love-Quotes.com, n.d.).

The appeal of the benign-violation theory comes in part from its consistency with the proposed evolutionary origins of humor in benign physical violations such as play fighting, which can also be seen in animals (Gervais & Wilson, 2005). The proponents of this theory argue that humor has a positive personal and social function in daily life; specifically, humor "provides a healthy and socially beneficial way to react to hypothetical threats, remote concerns, minor setbacks, social faux pas, cultural misunderstandings, and other benign violations people encounter on a regular basis" (McGraw & Warren, 2010, p. 1148). These theorists also argue that humor (e.g., laughter) is an important form of social communication, signaling that (benign) violations of social rules are often acceptable. In short, humor allows us to know that bending the social rules may be okay.

Another appeal of the benign-violation theory in the present context is that it suggests an additional reason why sexuality so often provides the content of humor: because it is fraught with rules, norms, and taboos. Thus, engaging in sex, regardless of the circumstances, will likely violate a social and moral guideline somewhere!

The importance of incongruity models of humor, such as benign-violation theory, cannot be overstated. Indeed, the ubiquity of some form of incongruous resolution in jokes makes benign-violation theory an appealing theory of humor in and of itself, even independent of tension theories; in fact, it is sometimes seen as a competing theory to tension-reduction models of humor (Smuts, 2009, April 12). However, these two theories of humor are perhaps more appropriately considered complementary, as they concentrate on two different elements of our mental/psychological life—cognitive and emotional, both of which are usually brought to bear by psychologists in explaining complex human behavior (see also the discussion in chapter 2 on the A, B, C, and Ds of sex). Incongruity models are "cognitive," dealing primarily with how we process information and knowledge. Thus, these theories concern our thoughts and their organization in the mind; how, for example, one bit of information is linked to another and how readily accessible it is to our consciousness. In contrast, tension-reduction models are more emotional in nature. They deal with our emotions and arousal. Sometimes these two elements are called the "cold" (cognitive) versus "hot" (emotional) elements of psychological life. So, let us assume that both elements—some level of hot (i.e., tension) and some level of cold (i.e., incongruity of ideas)—are important in humor.[4]

Okay, back to the Viagra joke and a more "cognitive" analysis: On a simple cognitive level, if you did not know that a penis becomes stiff and erect, that an erection is aided by Viagra, and that erections are often grasped (as in manual stimulation by a partner or in masturbation by boys and men themselves), then you would not "get" the joke. Since the man needs to grasp his own penis in this situation, knowledge of (and perhaps particularly the experience of) masturbation is also likely relevant. Now, if something is personally relevant, it is also likely to have some psychic tension associated with it. After all, most people—if not all—are a bit tense about and/or embarrassed by their masturbation experience, or at least were at one time in their lives. This raises an important point about how cognitive and emotional elements of mental processing operate in real life: they typically relate to and reinforce one another. Thus, if one has a cognitive "understanding" of the key elements of this joke (e.g., public masturbation), then one is also likely to have an emotional connection to these same elements.

From an incongruity perspective, understanding this joke needs to go beyond the mechanics of masturbation. Indeed, a rather sophisticated level of cognitive processing needs to occur in order for someone "to get" the joke. For example, a benign-violation humor theorist would likely argue that the Viagra joke is funny because we understand that two contradictory events have co-occurred: first, that grasping an erect penis in public is a violation of an important social code of conduct, and second, that this act in the present instance is only a benign violation, because it has been sanctioned by the dentist, presumably in the service of oral health. Someone who did not understand these two events, or who could not hold them in mind relatively simultaneously, would not "get" the joke.

Now let's consider an asexual person, who has no sexual attraction for others, and also perhaps no masturbation experience (in fact, no sexual interest whatsoever).[5] Would he or she laugh at the Viagra joke? Let's consider both emotional-tension and incongruity perspectives on humor.

From a straightforward emotional-tension perspective, I expect that an asexual person would not laugh, or at least would laugh less than an average sexual person. This is so because the asexual person can be assumed to have little or no tension about sexual matters generally, including about masturbation (e.g., no unused sexual arousal floating around, no masturbation guilt); after all, the asexual person has never had sex before and has no interest in it. Thus, there should be no emotional connection to this sexual activity and thus little psychic energy available to be discharged.

From a cognitive (i.e., incongruity) perspective, I expect that the asexual person would also have little self-relevant imagery of grasping an

erect penis—either his own (if a man) or a partner's. So, this information—an image of a man grasping a penis—should not be particularly
personally relevant and would not readily come to mind; thus, it is not
readily "cognitively accessible." Of course, the asexual person may have
imagined a scene such as this out of mild curiosity, or seen an image
before (e.g., on the Internet), but it should be less readily accessible to an
asexual person, relative to, say, a sexual man with a fair bit of masturbation experience.

However, using an analysis based on the benign-violation model, an
asexual person without masturbation experience may still understand
that grasping one's penis in public is a violation of an important social
rule. They would also understand that the dentist has sanctioned it, and
hence it is a benign violation. Thus, if knowledge of these two contradictory ideas occurs simultaneously, an asexual person may still appreciate
this joke.[6]

However, it is important to consider whether mere knowledge of
these two contradictory ideas is sufficient in this case to cause humor
appreciation, including laughter. As mentioned, perhaps this joke works
best, if at all, for those who very easily conjure up an image of a man
holding his erect penis (e.g., a man with a fair bit of masturbation experience).[7] Relative to a sexual person, an asexual person without such experience may be less cognitively "ready" to conjure up this image. Keep in
mind that jokes often work very quickly and require proper timing in
order for them to evoke appreciation (e.g., laughter). So, if the key elements of this joke—knowledge that public masturbation is occurring but
that it is a benign instance—are not brought into consciousness very
quickly, this joke is not likely to work. Moreover, people with sexual
experience (and masturbation experience, specifically) have likely rumi-
nated about what is and what is not "proper" sexual behavior (including
their own sexual behavior), and thus the idea or image of public masturbation may be readily known and hence readily accessible as a "violation." Thus, the likelihood of being able to access this information quickly
and hold it in mind simultaneously with the other key element of this
joke—that this instance is merely a benign violation—is probably increased by sexual experience.

Let us inject even more complexity into this analysis. As mentioned,
humor may be facilitated by a variety of tensions and motives, not just
sexual ones. Additional tensions are based on anger or fear. Freud and

others have argued that sarcastic humor, for example, utilizes the release of these more aggressive and fear-based tensions and motives. Thus, if someone is angry or resentful toward others (or perhaps just a bit scared of them), he or she may discharge this anger- or fear-based psychic tension by belittling them through sarcasm or other forms of aggressive humor. This type of humor puts enemies "in their place," or at least makes them less scary because they look silly, and not threatening. There is often anger- and fear-based tension associated with "out-groups," groups to which we do not belong or that are different from us. Relatedly, some theorists have championed "superiority" theories of humor, usually first associated with Thomas Hobbes (1840), who argued that self-esteem is often enhanced when experiencing the misfortunes of others. Thus, by a downward social comparison, we achieve a loftier place because someone else is belittled. More recently, social psychologists have co-opted elements of superiority theory to help explain some of the processes involved with the formation and defense of the social identity of a group. Humorous put-downs of an "out-group"—the group to which we do not belong—are sometimes enjoyable because they allow our group to achieve "positive distinctiveness," a sense of superiority that we, as a group, have a special distinction that sets us apart, and even above, other groups (Ferguson & Ford, 2008; Ruscher, 2001). Ethnic and gender-based ("sexist") jokes and put-downs are partially explained in this way (Ferguson & Ford, 2008).

How might this type of humor relate to asexuality? Some asexual people may have resentment toward and fear of the (majority) out-group—sexual people—just as some sexual people may have anger or resentment toward asexual people. Relatedly, our very sexualized society often places pressure on asexual people to have sex, perhaps causing tension in some asexual people, if not outright resentment of sexual people. If so, and if the Viagra joke somehow evokes an effective, belittling, and embarrassing image of a sexual person—a man being forced to grasp his erect penis in a dentist's office—one might argue that this joke could make an asexual person laugh.

SUMMARY

The ability of the Viagra joke, as in many sexual jokes, to create humor appreciation (i.e., laughter) may involve the use and release of sexual tension. The effectiveness of this joke may also involve the quick access-ibility of imagery related to a hand grasping an erect penis, along with, perhaps, this act being viewed as a benign violation of a social rule. As sexual people (particularly men with masturbation experience) should have the most sexual energy and tension, and the most experience asso-ciated with these images and ideas, this joke is especially relevant to and likely to be appreciated by them (compared to asexual people). However, there are many unknowns and complexities when it comes to under-standing humor, and it is possible that some circumstances (e.g., resent-ment of sexual people) may evoke humor appreciation for sexual jokes in asexual people.

My reasoning on asexuality and sexual humor in this chapter has been very speculative. The relationship between asexuality and sexual humor might be best described as an "empirical question"—that is, something that is unknown and needs to be studied.

Finally, I think a broad conclusion that should be drawn from this chapter is that sexuality is a pervasive part of most people's lives and is associated with considerable tensions and odd, even twisted, social rules, so much so that sexual content pervades one of the most important tools we use to negotiate social life: humor. Interestingly, if it turns out that asexual people do appreciate, even laugh at, sexual jokes (and I expect that many do), this may say more about our sexualized society and how everyone—sexual or not—is caught in its web of influence than it does about any hidden sexual motives of (self-identified) asexual people. Thus, the answer to the question posed earlier in this chapter—if a person who identifies as asexual laughs at a sexual joke, does this mean that he or she is sexual?—is *not necessarily*. It may just mean that he or she is also part of a sociocultural experience partially driven by sex. To end with, let me pose a related thought question that I took on and tried to answer in the context of art in chapter 11: What would our humor be like if we were an asexual species? With a domain of life so fraught with tension and social rules—sex—eliminated, would we be less *funny*?

NOTES

1. Some animals may have a form of rudimentary laughter (e.g., "proto-laughter" of chimps), or at least show some of the evolutionary physical precursors to laughter, such as excited and rhythmic physical behaviors (e.g., tail-wagging in dogs) (Eastman,

1936). There may also be some precursors of the often "rule-bending" element of humor in the play fighting of animals (Gervais & Wilson, 2005; see also later in this chapter).

2. It is popularly believed and has often been stated—in the Bible, in the popular media, and so on—that laughter is "good medicine." The implication of this widespread belief is that it must have evolved because of its physical health benefits. However, some theorists suggest that laughter's direct health benefits are minimal, or at least not yet sufficiently demonstrated. Instead, humor evolved because it had "social" benefits, easing social tension and allowing for smooth navigation among our fellow humans (Provine, 2000), and any health benefits are indirect and work through these social benefits (e.g., social support).

3. However, most modern theorists do not buy all of the elements of a classic tension-release model. Humor is not necessarily "cathartic" in the therapeutic sense; that is, it does not necessarily reduce the tendency to engage in future behaviors related to the tension (Ferguson & Ford, 2008; Martin, 2007). For example, research shows that sexist humor does not decrease the tendency to engage in sexist behavior soon afterward; sometimes the opposite occurs, and sexist humor may even lead to complex domineering behaviors (Hodson, Rush, & MacInnis, 2010). Thus, a straightforward catharsis model of humor based on sexual or other tension may not be correct. One alternative but related explanation for this kind of humor is that there may be a pleasantness associated with being able to release the tension of a repressed or suppressed impulse or motive, but such humor does not reduce our tendencies to engage in this impulse; it just releases us from the unpleasantness of not being able to express it. For example, modern social psychologists talk about disparagement humor of groups as releasing "negative intergroup motives" (Hodson, Rush, & MacInnis, 2010, p. 661).

4. Indeed, many modern theorists argue that humor is complex and multifaceted, and one usually needs both elements, especially when actual laughter occurs. Humor, broadly defined, does not always make us laugh; perhaps tension release is even required for actual laughter to occur. We may receive a rather pleasant feeling and perhaps a smile from, for example, a clever witticism, twist, or incongruity; yet it is still humor, even though it does not evoke the deep release of a joke that causes a belly laugh. But when humor does make us laugh, there is usually some level of tension involved and released.

5. Recall from the discussion of masturbation (chapter 5) that many asexual people do masturbate, but at a lower rate and less frequently than sexual people. If so, this analysis is, of course, most applicable to the non-masturbating asexuals.

6. If humor that causes laughter is more associated with emotional tension than other forms of humor (e.g., puns and other incongruities), then this joke may elicit only mild appreciation in asexual people. It may evoke a pleasant cognitive shift, a recognition of a strange incongruity being somewhat resolved. Thus, sexual people may laugh; asexual people may just smile?

7. So, yes, women (particularly those without much experience grasping a penis) may also not appreciate this joke.

THIRTEEN

Just Because

Have you been patiently reading along, but also wondering when I was going to address directly what you perceive to be the heart of the matter: the *cause(s)* of asexuality? If certain chapters touching on causes (e.g., chapter 6) only whetted your appetite for a more direct discussion of etiology, I can't blame you. Causes are important to people. They are not merely the preserve of adults—children are also fascinated by them. Sometimes children are so obsessed and unsatisfied when an adult answers their "why" question that it sets off a spiraling series of additional "but why" queries. So, finding out about the "cause" of an event merely prompts their curiosity about the cause behind this cause, and the cause behind that cause, and so on. After being beaten into submission by the barrage of questions, realizing that the child has a point and that the mysteries of the universe are often unknowable to children and adults alike, a parent may resort to the ambiguous, end-all answer: "Well, just because, dear. . . ."

Subdisciplines of philosophy and psychology are devoted to how we determine causes—how we know what we know in *epistemology* (philosophy), and how we attribute causes, including laying blame, in *attribution theory* (psychology). Indeed, social psychologists suggest that we are not only obsessed with causes but also prone to bias in our thinking about them. I raise this issue because even we scientists may forward a cause that reflects bias. Keep that in mind as you read along!

What is a cause? We may think of a cause as something that gives rise to an event or phenomenon. In other words, causes deal with the *hows and whys* of events. But causes are complicated, and not just because, as social psychologists suggest, humans have bias in the way they make attributions. Often phenomena have multiple causes. So, for example, asexuality may be caused by both a biological event (e.g., prenatal hormones permanently organizing a site in the lower brain) and an environmental one (e.g., no exposure to sexualizing social forces, such as randy peers).[1] Sometimes causes are interactive or conditional; that is, they only occur in one circumstance but not others. So, perhaps a lack of sexualizing social forces has a profound effect on one individual because he or she is predisposed to these forces, but a lack of sexualizing social forces in another individual has no impact, because he or she does not have a susceptible predisposition; in the latter case, the individual would be sexual regardless of these sexualizing social forces or the lack of them.

Causes can also be distinguished by their level of analysis: micro versus macro. *Micro* refers to causes within an individual, including at the very basic cellular level (e.g., the organization of brain cells). Biological and some psychological causes are focused on the micro level. *Macro* refers to causes that are broader or more societally focused (e.g., socioeconomic status as a determinant of one's social environment). Some psychological, sociological, and historical causes are macro focused. Of course, an academic usually prefers one type of cause over the other—be it either micro or macro—because one type of cause usually fits more comfortably within his or her own discipline than the other. However, it is very important to remember that macro and micro causes are not necessarily in competition with one another for understanding reality. A macro cause may be compatible with or related to a micro one. For example, socioeconomic status (macro cause) may influence the environmental conditions to which a mother is exposed, which may, in turn, raise or lower hormone levels in her womb, affecting a fetus's brain development (micro cause) and its propensity to asexuality.

Also, we can focus on causes at different spots along a very long timeline. Some causes are more immediate or proximal in nature; that is, closer in time to the event itself. Most causes offered up by biologists, psychologists, and sociologists are of this nature. Some causes are distal in nature—that is, further away in time from the event itself. Causes from a historical or evolutionary perspective can be distal in nature. Historical causes can be considered distal because they occurred in the distant past, perhaps many centuries ago. Evolutionary explanations are distal because they concentrate on why a phenomenon, such as asexuality within humans, may have evolved during a time in the natural history of the species, and/or why this phenomenon may have conferred an adaptive advantage (or at least not a disadvantage) across time. Some causes are so distal as to be construable as "ultimate." Thus, one might argue that the Big Bang or God is the ultimate or first cause of everything, including human asexuality. Such ultimate causes may be correct in a broad sense, but they are often not particularly useful in the science of understanding current events or in understanding differences between people in the here and now.[2]

I have already mentioned two distal causes of asexuality. In chapter 3, I suggested that some historical eras—for example, the Victorian era in Britain—may have caused elevated rates of asexuality in certain individuals (e.g., upper-class women). One could expand on such distal explanations, if one were a historian (which I am not), and do an in-depth analysis of different eras and their roles in causing different prevalence rates of asexuality.[3]

Another relatively distal cause of asexuality is the evolutionary process. One of the great evolutionary puzzles of sexology, aside from why sex exists (see chapter 3), is why homosexuality exists, given that it is partly genetically based and has existed over time and across cultures. As I discussed in chapter 11, the answer may have to do with kin selection. If, for example, a "man-loving" gene is expressed not only in a gay man but also in his female relatives, it may confer a reproductive advantage on the latter, making his sisters particularly fertile and thus increasing the replication of the family's genes. Alternatively, a gay gene (i.e., a genetic predisposition to same-sex attraction) may be of some advantage to an individual because, under certain environmental circumstances, it may be associated with helping relatives' children (e.g., nephews and nieces) survive and reproduce. In both cases, then, "gay genes" may exist because they serve to replicate one's broader gene pool (i.e., kin).

Asexuality may also be an evolutionary puzzle in need of a solution, assuming it also has a genetic basis across time. Perhaps asexuality "genes" are also conserved throughout evolutionary time because of kin-selection mechanisms. Thus, it would be interesting to examine in a research study if asexual people give, on average, elevated care for their siblings' children, thus potentially offsetting their reduced sexual reproduction by such kin-enhancement strategies.[4]

Speaking of genetics and asexuality, no studies thus far have tested for this linkage directly. Indirect evidence is all we can rely on at this point: no studies have ever examined asexuality as a trait and its "concordance" or similarity between identical (as compared to fraternal) twins, a common methodology used to determine if variation in a trait is partly genetically based. Moreover, no one has ever isolated a specific gene directly associated with asexuality.

But let's discuss some plausible genetic candidates affecting asexuality. In chapter 6, we discussed the role of certain X-linked (female) or Y-linked (male) genes in sexual differentiation. Some of these genes may play a key role in the prenatal development of the brain. Some of these gene effects on prenatal development are also independent of hormonal effects. In other words, they may directly affect the structure or organization of brain cells associated with sexual attraction. These genes, however, are not well studied. Some other sex-linked genes are well studied and have been clearly shown to affect hormones and their impact on sexual differentiation. For example, the SRY gene allows for the development of the testes, which produce hormones during prenatal and postnatal development. There are also other "hormone-related" genes. For example, the androgen receptor (AR) gene is important in determining how hormones affect the body and the brain. As you may recall, receptors are specialized parts of the cell that receive and activate a hormone molecule, and androgens (testosterone in particular) affect sex drive and prenatally organize sites in the lower brain related to gender, sexuality, and attraction. Variation in the AR gene likely affects the person's level of sensitivity to testosterone. Interestingly, variation in the AR gene has been implicated in male-to-female transsexualism (Hare et al., 2009), and there is evidence that asexuality is associated with elevated rates of atypical gender identity (see also chapter 6). There is also evidence that variation in the AR gene might influence the age at which puberty begins (Comings, Muhleman, Johnson, & MacMurray, 2002), and there is evidence that the age of first menstruation (menarche) is, on average, later in asexual women than in sexual women (Bogaert, 2004). Finally, one of the explanations for asexuality in animals is an alteration in the receptors for testosterone (see also chapter 3). In sum, this research suggests that variations in the AR gene may underlie (or least predispose someone to) asexuality.

Genes underlying receptors for other hormones, including estrogens (e.g., estradiol), may also be involved in the causes of asexuality. Estrogens, among other functions, help regulate women's menstrual cycle,[5] but also likely play some role in the sexual differentiation of both male and female fetuses. There is also some evidence that male-to-female transsexuals have an atypical variation in the estrogen receptor (ER) gene (Henningsson et al., 2005).

Recall from chapter 6 that sexual differentiation involves the development of female features (feminization) and male features (masculinization), as well as processes that prevent or remove female features in male fetuses (de-feminization) and prevent or remove male features in female fetuses (de-masculinization). Exploration of the possible role of androgen and/or estrogen receptors in the sexual differentiation process raises the possibility that some asexual people are, partially, neither *masculinized* nor *feminized* (see also chapter 6). In other words, instead of an inversion of masculinization and feminization that, at times, may occur in gays and lesbians during prenatal development (Ellis & Ames, 1987), some asexual people may be *de-gendered* during prenatal development. That asexual people report a high level of atypical gender identity, along with the role of these hormone receptor genes in transsexualism, adds support for this possibility.

Genes are chemicals that provide the codes for proteins, the building blocks of life, which in turn produce parts of the body (e.g., hormones, receptors, and/or brain sites); thus, variations in certain genes may alter typical brain development and affect asexuality. But aside from genes, are there other factors that could cause alterations in typical development of the brain? There are, and these factors have broad applicability to sexual orientation development, including the development of an asexual orientation. Let's first consider these factors in the context of traditional sexual orientation—that is, in the development of a homosexual versus a heterosexual orientation.

One biological theory of sexual orientation is that homosexuality results when atypical events during pregnancy expose fetuses to variations in prenatal hormones (e.g., Ellis & Ames, 1987). These atypical events may include unusual pregnancies (e.g., carrying twins), a maternal exposure to certain drugs, or stress during pregnancy. Such events may alter the typical hormonal milieu (e.g., raise or lower testosterone levels) of the womb during pregnancy, and consequently alter the course of fetal brain development.

Another biological theory of male homosexuality is that atypical events during pregnancy expose male fetuses to a maternal immune response. In this theory, some pregnant mothers have an immune reaction to a substance important in male fetal development (Blanchard & Bogaert, 1996; Bogaert & Skorska, 2011). For example, male fetuses, because of genes on their Y-chromosome, produce certain male-specific proteins that may be seen as "foreign" to the mother. Thus, the target of a mother's immune response may be these proteins, some of which are expressed on the surface of male fetal brain cells. Products of a mother's immune system (e.g., antibodies) might alter the typical function of these proteins and thus alter their role in typical sexual differentiation, leading some males later in life to be attracted to men as opposed to women.

What could cause such an immune reaction, and what factors affect the degree to which such an immune reaction alters the typical development of the fetus? The events mentioned above—unusual pregnancies—may be relevant. For example, some unusual pregnancies may lead to a higher likelihood of products of the mother's immune system (e.g., antibodies) crossing the placental barrier that separates the fetus and the mother, ultimately affecting fetal development.

In summary, two biological theories of sexual orientation development—variations in prenatal hormones and a maternal immune response—have as a central theme that an atypical womb environment can predispose fetuses to homosexuality. Yet there is often no direct information about atypical events that occurred while a fetus developed in its mother's womb. A mother may know this about her pregnancy history, but her sons and daughters, when asked in research studies, may not be privy to this information. Moreover, even if there is information about such atypical events, very often little direct evidence exists that these events sufficiently altered the womb environment—such as by producing atypical hormone levels or a maternal immune response—to affect fetal development.

Because direct evidence of such changes is rarely available, researchers often seek indirect "markers" of biological development, particularly those markers that are determined before birth and that are sensitive to atypical womb conditions. One of the most important and well-studied biological markers of prenatal development is handedness.

Did you know that fetuses often suck their thumbs? They do, and ultrasound studies show that the rate of right-handed thumb sucking in fetuses matches relatively closely the rate of right-handedness in adults (Hepper, Shabidullah, & White, 1991). This rather intriguing correspondence in bodily characteristics between fetal and adult life suggests that handedness is determined before birth.

Handedness is linked to genes (and what isn't?), including the androgen receptor (AR) gene mentioned above (Medland et al., 2005). Elevated non-right-handedness is also associated with atypical pregnancy/birth conditions (e.g., birth stress) (Coren, 1993). Handedness is additionally linked to variations in prenatal hormone levels (Witelson & Nowakowski, 1991). Thus, if a group has a rate of non-right-handedness that differs statistically from, say, 10 percent—the rate seen in many adult populations—it suggests that this group has elevated variations in relevant genes and/or atypical prenatal development (e.g., altered hormone levels). For example, non-right-handedness is elevated in gay men and lesbians (Lalumière, Blanchard, & Zucker, 2000) and other groups with atypical sexual attractions (Bogaert, 2001).[6] This research suggests that atypical womb events (e.g., variations in prenatal hormones) can alter brain mechanisms affecting both handedness and patterns of sexual attraction in these groups. As such, handedness is also an important biological marker to examine in the context of a possible biological underpinning of asexuality.

Is there any evidence that asexuals have atypical handedness patterns? There is. Perhaps the most intriguing finding related to the etiology of asexuality is that 26 percent of (self-identified) asexual people have been found to be non-right-handed (Yule, 2011). This is a very high percentage in comparison to population norms or to the control group of heterosexual participants (12 percent) in the study itself. The elevated non-right-handedness occurred in both asexual men and asexual women, and is consistent with elevated rates of non-right-handedness in both gay men and lesbians (Lalumière et al., 2000).

Another potential biological marker of atypical prenatal development is a high number of older brothers. Such a marker is relevant to the biology of men's sexual orientation and the theory of maternal immune response contributing to male homosexuality mentioned above. An important corollary of this theory is that the immune effect should have a higher likelihood of occurring with each son that a mother gestates. This is because a mother has increased opportunities to develop an immune response against male-specific substances with each male gestation. Each male fetus gestated increases the likelihood that eventually a mother will be exposed to and ultimately react against such a substance as a male-specific protein. So, in other words, we should observe an "older brother effect"—a greater number of older brothers in gay men versus heterosexual men—if a maternal immune effect underlies male homosexuality. There should also be no sibling (e.g., older sister) effect in female homosexuality, because a mother should not develop an immune response against a female-specific substance, given that she herself is female.

Is there an older brother effect in gay men? Yes! On average, gay men have a higher number of older brothers than do heterosexual men. In 1996, psychologist Ray Blanchard and I first demonstrated this effect using a Canadian sample (Blanchard & Bogaert, 1996). However, there is now a large body of research, including cross-cultural studies, showing this effect, but only in men's sexual orientation (Blanchard, 2004; Bogaert & Skorska, 2011). The fact that this "older brother effect" is indeed a *biological* phenomenon is further demonstrated by research showing that gay men have an elevated number of older *biological* brothers, even ones with whom they were not reared; yet they do not have an elevated number of older stepbrothers or adopted brothers (Bogaert, 2006a). Thus, these findings point to the importance of the biological mother, whom biological siblings share, and not the childhood or rearing environment, which step- or adopted siblings share when they were raised together.

Interestingly, there is recent evidence of an "older brother effect" in asexual men: Morag Yule (2011), in her master's thesis under the supervision of psychologist Lori Brotto at the University of British Columbia, found that asexual men have a higher number of older brothers than a comparison sample of heterosexual men. No one yet has conducted a study on whether the older brother effect in asexual men is restricted to biological (versus non-biological) older brothers, but the pattern of sibling effects in the Yule study is very similar to those observed in many similar studies of male homosexuality.

The discussion above places a heavy emphasis on prenatal mechanisms, such as hormones organizing brain structures during fetal development.[7] What about current or circulating hormones affecting asexuality? Do asexual people have low circulating hormones that reduce sex drive, and minimize their sexual attractions?

As mentioned in chapter 2, prior to the 1970s, gay men were sometimes administered high levels of testosterone. This was done because "reparative-oriented" clinicians felt that this hormone treatment could change gay men's orientation. Yet it did not make them attracted to women; it just made them horny for more sex with men! The problem with this approach, aside from the ethics of it, was that gay men's orientation was already determined, perhaps even before birth, and thus administering testosterone in adolescence and adulthood just "activated" or stimulated their sex drives. So the testosterone worked like fuel on the fire of whatever disposition (i.e., brain organization) was already there in the first place.

By the same token, it is unlikely that we can change many asexual people's orientation by administering sex hormones. Thus, like gay men, asexual people's underlying attractions (to no one, in this case) are unlikely to be changed by such interventions, although they may make the masturbating asexuals masturbate even more (see chapter 5)! Indeed, the fact that some asexual people are masturbating already (and some do so frequently) means that, at least for these asexual people, their asexuality is not a sex-drive issue, and thus their underlying sexual connection to others is unlikely to change with added hormones. Finally, as mentioned in chapter 3, there is little evidence that asexuality in animals (the so-called duds in rodents or NORs in rams) is the result of low levels of circulating or activating hormones (Adkins-Reagan, 2005; Perkins, Fitzgerald, & Price, 1992).[8]

People often suggest to me that there *must* be a childhood event—such as sexual abuse or other trauma—that causes asexuality. Given my hefty list of possible biological explanations reviewed above, perhaps you assume that I dismiss these suggestions, if only in a polite, Canadian kind of way? Well, no, I don't. I believe that at times asexuality is affected by, or at least predisposed to occur because of, atypical childhood events.

Research suggests that some atypical sexual attractions partly result from atypical rearing events, including sexual abuse (Seto, 2008). This fact raises the possibility that asexuality—as it is also an unusual form of sexual attraction—may be caused by such events. These traumatic events may be experienced very negatively and disrupt any sexual interest or attraction that normally arises in an individual. Thus, traumatic events could shut down an emerging sexuality. These events may also be coupled with (or interact with) other predisposing factors—such as prenatal influences—that could seal the deal on an individual's asexuality.

However, there is no direct evidence that sexual abuse causes asexuality. We must also be cautious about overstating the role of sexual abuse in the etiology of atypical sexual attractions, as many people exposed to such abuse—traumatic as it may be at the time—will not develop an unusual sexuality or other long-term consequences (Rellini & Meston, 2007; Rind, Tromovitch, & Bauserman, 1998).

Recall that one of the themes of this book is that asexuality is a diverse phenomenon. The diverse patterns of asexuality are often gender related, with men likely to show one pattern, and women to show another. Masturbation experience is a good example of how the diversity in asexuality people is often gender related: Only some asexual people masturbate, and they tend to be men. Women may thus be more likely than men to be asexual, because the former are less likely to masturbate (see chapter 6). Masturbation may act as "conditioning" trials leading to the development of strong, enduring attractions to others, particularly if the masturbation is paired with images of others. Thus, another environmental influence affecting the development of asexuality may be a lack of early sexual experimentation (i.e., childhood/adolescent masturbation with fantasy). Consistent with this view, some theorists have argued that sexual attraction to others results from arousal experiences—including masturbation—directed at or with others (Storms, 1981).

Sexual attraction may also emerge from exposure to and familiarity with same-sex or opposite-sex peers (Bem, 1996). If, for example, a boy's gender identity and role are traditional—for instance, engaging in traditional "masculine" behaviors, such as rough-and-tumble play and sports with other boys—girls may become "exotic" and hence, ultimately, sexually arousing. Thus, the boy may develop permanent attractions to the erotically charged opposite sex.

But what if this boy has little contact with and no identification with peers? Would this boy's dis-identification with both sexes create, at least in some, an ambivalence to both and, hence, a sexual disinterest in all people later on life—that is, asexuality?

At this point, the role of the environment in asexual development, including childhood events (e.g., trauma), masturbation, and peers—remain a mystery. Research on asexual people has collected only basic information on their social environments: education, ethnicity, and social class (Bogaert, 2004; Bogaert, in press-a). Yet this information, limited as it may be, suggests that some asexual people have been exposed to an atypical environment relative to a standard, white, middle- or upper-class environment occurring in most Western societies. Asexual people are, on average, more likely to come from lower-class homes than sexual people. They are also somewhat lower in education, relative to sexual people. Finally, asexual people are, on average, more likely to have a nonwhite ethnicity than sexual people. Are these circumstances a proxy for unusual social circumstances during childhood and adolescence? Could they have an impact on sexual development through, say, increased exposure to some traumatic events that occur disproportionately in some lower-class homes, or perhaps through fewer peer interactions as a result of less school-based education? Could ethnic differences between asexual and sexual people indicate that some asexual people have been not been "acculturated" to a sexualized Western society (Brotto, Chik, Ryder, Gorzalka, & Seal, 2005)? These questions are intriguing but remain unanswered and await further research.

SUMMARY

One of the themes of this book is that the study of asexuality informs our understanding of sexuality. This is also true in the case of etiology. Prenatal mechanisms (e.g., genes, hormones, maternal immune response) potentially underlying asexuality may be the same ones that underlie traditional sexual orientations (gay, straight, and bisexual), and sexual variability generally. Thus, to have some understanding of one is to have some understanding of the other. This also holds true for nonbiological influences on sexuality. For example, peers and masturbation (and the role of conditioning) may play some role in sexualizing or de-sexualizing a person, depending on how these influences play themselves out in the individual.

You could say that I am an expert on sexual orientation development, as my research work in this area is well published and some of it is well known (e.g., on the older brother effect in men's sexual orientation). So, as an expert (ahem!), I guess I am permitted some bold, concluding statements about the causes of sexual attractions, including the origins of asexuality. But I won't make such a bold statement about causes, because, as mentioned at the beginning of this chapter, I know that causes are tricky and complex things. For example, the etiology of asexuality may reflect multiple and interactive influences, both biological and environmental in origin. This etiology may also be best understood by resorting to both distal and proximal causes and both macro and micro influences. In addition, I hesitate to be bold because I know that the research on asexuality is just beginning. Thus, although there is tantalizing research (mostly of a proximate, micro nature), along with some intriguing speculations, regarding the origins of asexuality, we do not know what causes someone to develop as an asexual person. So, if you are asked why asexuality exists, and you reply, "Well, just because," I suppose I would not blame you.

NOTES

1. Of course, when a phenomenon has multiple causes—say, two, for this example—they could be two discrete biological causes, or two discrete environmental ones, and not necessarily one of each.

2. Like micro and macro causes, distal and proximate causes are not necessarily incompatible, as they can also coexist at different points along a (potentially very long) causal stream or pathway for a given phenomenon. For example, an evolutionary cause of gender differences in sexuality is that during human evolution, men and women developed different mating strategies. Women developed a more cautious mating strategy to maximize their large parental/reproductive investment (relatively few eggs, nine months of gestation). Men developed a more risky and indiscriminate mating strategy to maximize their small parental/reproductive investment (cheap, replaceable sperm). A compatible proximate explanation is that these different mating strategies are caused by hormone levels affecting sex drive, with women exhibiting lower levels of testosterone and a lower sex drive than men. Sometimes evolutionary causes are construed as the *whys*, and proximate causes as the *hows*, of events and phenomena.

3. As mentioned, historical causes would also constitute more of a macro- than a microanalysis.

4. This is not to imply that this would be a "conscious" strategy.

5. Estrogens (e.g., estradiol) are sometimes referred to as "female hormones," but this is a bit simplistic, just as suggesting that testosterone is a male hormone (see the complexity of sex and gender in chapter 6). For example, testosterone itself can be converted to estradiol under the influence of an enzyme (aromatase) and both testosterone and estrogen (e.g., estradiol) are produced in both males and females.

6. One of these groups is pedophiles. This fact should not be taken to mean that homosexuality (or asexuality) and thus pedophilia should be seen as linked in a behavioral way—that is, to mean that gay men, lesbians, or asexuals are more likely to abuse children. This is not the case. Instead, this fact should be taken as evidence that sexual attraction, atypical and otherwise, is very likely influenced by prenatal events.

7. We can add to this evidence the research mentioned in chapter 6 showing that asexual women have atypical menarche onset (Bogaert, 2004). There is also evidence that asexual people may be somewhat shorter than sexual people (Bogaert, 2004). Atypical menarche and stature are both potential markers of altered biological devel-

opment, including an altered prenatal development. Interestingly, there is evidence of atypical height patterns in gays and lesbians, although this research is not consistent and may be subject to non-biological interpretations (Bogaert & McCreary, 2011).

8. Does this mean that no asexual person would ever become sexual (e.g., develop sexual attractions) by taking testosterone? Not necessarily. Although the majority of asexual people likely do not have a "hormone deficiency," there is always a possibility that some asexual people have lower-than-average testosterone or other hormones relative to sexual people. For example, low hormone levels in some asexual people may occur because of a health condition (for some evidence of this, see my original article published in 2004). Also, it is possible that some asexual people with average hormone levels who take abnormally high testosterone could raise their sex drive and, perhaps, develop some level of sexual attraction for others. There are at least two issues here, though: First, as mentioned, there is currently little evidence that asexual people, as a whole, have lower testosterone levels than average sexual people. Second, is it ethical to administer abnormally high hormones to an asexual person if asexuality, arguably, is not a disorder (see also chapters 8 and 9)?

FOURTEEN

The Beginning

We have reached the end of this book. Have I converted you from a sexual person to an asexual one, or from an asexual person to a sexual one? You may be laughing at this point, as I expect you know that I asked this question tongue-in-cheek. After all, our sexual attractions, or lack of them, are not easily swayed. Thus, whatever mysteries give rise to them (see chapter 13), once they are laid down, they don't change easily.

This book was intended for a broad audience: anyone interested in understanding asexuality, and anyone interested in taking a view of human sexuality through a new lens. Toward that end, in chapter 2 I explored the constructs underlying the psychology of sexuality, which allowed us to define asexuality as a lack of sexual attraction. Exploring these constructs also provided insight into the nature of sexuality by defining its borders and revealing how related constructs such as romance and love can be decoupled from it. I also explored the biological and cultural history of asexuality in chapter 3. What do an amoeba, a famous mathematician, and Jughead Jones have in common? In chapter 4, I presented information on the prevalence of asexuality. The concern about the number of humans in various sexual groups reveals the fascination with our place on the sexual spectrum. In chapter 5, I discussed the rather delicate subject of masturbation and how it is important to understanding variation in asexuality. Later, in chapter 10, I presented evidence that some forms of asexuality in which masturbation co-occurs with persistent fantasy may constitute a paraphilia, or an unusual form of sexual attraction. I even named a new paraphilia! In chapter 6, I probed that mystery of mysteries, female sexual desire, and explored how men and women differ in their expression of sexuality, including asexuality. The forging of an asexual identity, and how it relates to the development of all identities (sexual and otherwise), was presented in chapter 7. In chapters 8 and 9, I asked the question "Is there one right way to live a human life?" My answer, after surveying the scene and trundling out a few arguments, was "no"; thus, if one is content as an asexual person, then one is probably better off than many people (if not the majority) who live in the sexualized modern Western world. Asexuality is a complex phenomenon and not easily framed as a mental problem; indeed, the case could be made that sexuality, not asexuality, is a form of madness! In chapters 11 and 12, I explored our sexual planet, and how sex is a pervasive, even insidious, influence on our lives. The examples I chose to illustrate this point were art, food, and humor, but other domains of human life are equally open to sexual analysis.

I hope that you have seen sexuality in a new light by reading this book. I have by writing it. This book has distilled for me much of the knowledge I have gained in my career as a sex educator and researcher, and I now see sexuality through a new lens because of my research on asexuality.

Finally, a few words on the title of this brief, concluding chapter: Is it truly *a beginning*? Not really, as there is already a small but important body of literature on asexuality, along with a plethora of literature that allows us to view sexuality for what I believe it is: the great, but utterly mad, story of human life. But the conclusion of this book is still more of a beginning than an end, because the thought and work devoted to understanding asexuality and its strange counterpart, sexuality, is in its early stages. Take this book and its concluding chapter as an invitation—the party hasn't yet started.

Bibliography

1-Love-Quotes.com. (n.d.). Kate O'Brien quotes. Retrieved May 19, 2011, from www.1-love-quotes.com/quote/927500

10percent.com. (n.d.). Retrieved from www.10percent.com

Abbott, E. (2001). *The history of celibacy.* New York: Da Capo Press.

Adkins-Reagan, E. (2005). *Hormones and animal social behavior.* Princeton, NJ: Princeton University Press.

Allport, G. W. (1954). *The nature of prejudice.* Cambridge, MA: Perseus Books.

American Psychiatric Association. (1980). *Diagnostic and statistical manual of mental disorders* (3rd ed.). Washington, DC: Author.

American Psychiatric Association. (2000). *Diagnostic and statistical manual of mental disorders* (4th ed., text rev.). Washington, DC: Author.

AnyOtherName. (2010, August 22). But . . . I don't WANT to masturbate . . . [Online forum post]. Retrieved from www.asexuality.org/en/index.php?/topic/53785-but-i-dont-want-to-masturbate

Arnold, A. P. (2004). Sex chromosomes and brain gender. *Nature Reviews Neuroscience, 5,* 701–708. doi:10.1038/nrn1494

Associated Press. (2007, December 3). Gay neighborhoods worry about losing identity. *Life on MSNBC.com.* Retrieved from www.msnbc.msn.com/id/17583200/ns/us_news-life/t/gay-neighborhoods-worry-about-losing-identity#.TjtNF3O4IXw

Bailey, J. M., Dunne, M. P., & Martin, N. G. (2000). Genetic and environmental influences on sexual orientation and its correlates in an Australian twin sample. *Journal of Personality and Social Psychology, 78,* 524–536. doi:10.1037/0022-3514.78.3.524

Bakker, J. (2003). Sexual differentiation of the neuroendocrine mechanisms regulating mate recognition in mammals. *Journal of Neuroendocrinology, 15,* 615–621. doi:10.1046/j.1365-2826.2003.01036.x

Baumeister, R. F. (2000). Gender differences in erotic plasticity: The female sex drive as socially flexible and responsive. *Psychological Bulletin, 126,* 347–374. doi:10.1037/0033-2909.126.3.347

Baumeister, R. F., Catanese, K. R., & Vohs, K. D. (2001). Is there a gender difference in strength of sex drive? Theoretical views, conceptual distinctions, and a review of relevant evidence. *Personality and Social Psychology Review, 5,* 242–273. doi:10.1207/S15327957PSPR0503_5

Baumle, A. (Ed.). (in press). *International handbook on the demography of sexuality.* New York: Springer Press.

Bell, G. (1982). *The masterpiece of nature: The evolution and genetics of sexuality.* Berkeley: University of California Press.

Bem, D. J. (1996). Exotic becomes erotic: A developmental theory of sexual orientation. *Psychological Review, 103*(2), 320–335. doi:10.1037//0033-295X.103.2.320

Benjamin, H. (1966). *The transsexual phenomenon.* New York: Julian Press.

Berrill, K. T. (1992). Anti-gay violence and victimization in the United States: An overview. In G. M. Herek & K. T. Berrill (Eds.), *Hate crimes: Confronting violence against lesbians and gay men* (pp. 19–45). Newbury Park, CA: Sage.

Billy, J. O. G., Tanfer, K., Grady, W. R., & Klepinger, D. H. (1993). The sexual behavior of men in the United States. *Family Planning Perspectives, 25*, 52–60. Retrieved from www.jstor.org/stable/2136206

Blanchard, R. (1989). The concept of autogynephilia and the typology of male gender dysphoria. *Journal of Nervous and Mental Disease, 177*, 616–623. doi:10.1097/00005053-198910000-00004

Blanchard, R. (1991). Clinical observations and systematic studies of autogynephilia. *Journal of Sex & Marital Therapy, 17*, 235–251. Retrieved from www.tandf.co.uk/journals/titles/0092623X.asp

Blanchard, R. (1993). The she-male phenomenon and the concept of partial autogynephilia. *Journal of Sex & Marital Therapy, 19*, 69–76. Retrieved from www.tandf.co.uk/journals/titles/0092623X.asp

Blanchard, R. (2004). Quantitative and theoretical analyses of the relation between older brothers and homosexuality in men. *Journal of Theoretical Biology, 230*, 173–187.

Blanchard, R., & Bogaert, A. F. (1996). Homosexuality in men and number of older brothers. *American Journal of Psychiatry, 153*, 27–31.

Bogaert, A. F. (1996). Volunteer bias in males: Evidence for both personality and sexuality differences. *Archives of Sexual Behavior, 25*, 125–140. doi:10.1007/BF02437932

Bogaert, A. F. (2001). Handedness, criminality, and sexual offending. *Neuropsychologia, 39*, 465–469.

Bogaert, A. F. (2003). Number of older brothers and sexual orientation: New tests and the attractive/behavior distinction in two national probability samples. *Journal of Personality and Social Psychology, 84*, 644–652. doi:10.1037/0022-3514.84.3.644

Bogaert, A. F. (2004). Asexuality: Prevalence and associated factors in a national probability sample. *Journal of Sex Research, 41*(3), 279–287. doi:10.1080/00224490409552235

Bogaert, A. F. (2006a). Biological versus nonbiological older brothers and men's sexual orientation. *Proceedings of the National Academy of Sciences (PNAS), 103*, 10771–10774.

Bogaert, A. F. (2006b). Toward a conceptual understanding of asexuality. *Review of General Psychology, 10*, 241–250. doi:10.1037/1089-2680.10.3.241

Bogaert, A. F. (2008). Asexuality: Dysfunction or variation. In J. M. Caroll & M. K. Alena (Eds.), *Psychological sexual dysfunctions* (pp. 9–13). New York: Nova Biomedical Books.

Bogaert, A. F. (in press-a). Asexuality: Prevalence and associated factors in NATSAL-II. In A. Baumle (Ed.), *International handbook on the demography of sexuality*. New York: Springer Press.

Bogaert, A. F. (in press-b). Asexuality and autochorissexualism (identity-less sexuality). *Archives of Sexual Behavior*.

Bogaert, A. F., & Brotto, L. (in progress). *Object of desire self-consciousness theory*.

Bogaert, A. F., & Hafer, C. L. (2009). Predicting the timing of coming out in gay and bisexual men from world beliefs, physical attractiveness, and childhood gender identity/role. *Journal of Applied Social Psychology, 39*, 1991–2019. doi:10.1111/j.1559-1816.2009.00513.x

Bogaert, A. F., & McCreary, D. (2011). Self-reported height and masculine sex roles. *Sex Roles, 65*, 548–556.

Bogaert, A. F., & Skorska, M. (2011). Sexual orientation, fraternal birth order, and the maternal immune hypothesis: A review. *Frontiers in Neuroendocrinology, 32,* 247–254.

Bogaert, A. F., Visser, B. A., Pozzebon, J., & Wanless, J. (2011). Women's fantasies and their language of love: The role of object of desire self-consciousness. Poster presented at SSSS (Western Division), San Francisco, California.

Boyd, R., & Richerson, P. J. (1985). *Culture and the evolutionary process.* Chicago: University of Chicago Press.

Broad, G. (2010, February 28). Athletes [Web log post]. Retrieved from http://measureofdoubt.blogspot.com/2010/02/athletes.html

Brotto, L., Chik, H., Ryder, A. G., Gorzalka, B., & Seal, B. N. (2005). Acculturation and sexual function in Asian women. *Archives of Sexual Behavior, 34,* 613–626.

Brotto, L. A., Knudson, G., Inskip, J., Rhodes, K., & Erskine, Y. (2010). Asexuality: A mixed methods approach. *Archives of Sexual Behavior, 39,* 599–618. doi:10.1007/s10508-008-9434-x

Brotto, L. A., & Yule, M. A. (2011). Physiological and subjective sexual arousal in self-identified asexual women. *Archives of Sexual Behavior, 40,* 699–712. doi:10.1007/s10508-010-9671-7

Bulwa, D. (2009, August 24). Asexuals leave the closet, find community. *SF Gate.* Retrieved from www.sfgate.com/cgi-bin/article.cgi?f=/c/a/2009/08/24/MNC6194GN4.DTL

Buss, D. M., & Schmitt, D. P. (1993). Sexual strategies theory: An evolutionary perspective on human mating. *Psychological Review, 100,* 204–232. doi:10.1037//0033-295X.100.2.204

Busseri, M., Willoughby, T., Chalmers, H., & Bogaert, A. F. (2006). Same-sex attraction and successful adolescent development. *Journal of Youth and Adolescence, 35,* 563–575. doi:10.1007/s10964-006-9071-4

Byrne, D. (1977). Social psychology and the study of sexual behavior. *Personality and Social Psychology Bulletin, 3,* 3–30. doi:10.1177/014616727600300102

Caine-Bish, N., & Scheule, B. (2009). Gender differences in food preferences of school-aged children and adolescents. *Journal of School Health, 79,* 532–540. doi:10.1111/j.1746-1561.2009.00445.x

Cameron, L., & Rutland, A. (2006). Extended contact through story reading in school: Reducing children's prejudice toward the disabled. *Journal of Social Issues, 62,* 469–488. doi:10.1111/j.1540-4560.2006.00469.x

Cantor, J., Blanchard, R., & Barbaree, H. (2009). Sexual disorders. In P. H. Blaney & T. Millon (Eds.), *Oxford textbook of psychopathology* (pp. 527–548). New York: Oxford University Press.

Cantor, J. M. (2011). New MRI studies support the Blanchard typology of male-to-female transsexualism. *Archives of Sexual Behavior.* Advance online publication. doi:10.1007/s10508-011-9805-6

Carré, J. M., Putnam, S. K., & McCormick, C. M. (2009). Testosterone responses to competition predict future aggressive behaviour at a cost to reward in men. *Psychoneuroendocrinology, 34,* 561–570. doi:10.1016/j.psyneuen.2008.10.018

Carroll, L., & Tenniel, J. (1960). *Alice's adventures in wonderland, and Through the looking-glass.* New York: New American Library.

Cash, T. F., Morrow, J. A., Hrabosky, J. I., & Perry, A. A. (2004). How has body image changed? A cross-sectional investigation of college women and men from 1983 to

2001. *Journal of Consulting and Clinical Psychology, 72*, 1081–1089. doi:10.1037/0022-006X.72.6.1081

Cass, V. C. (1979). Homosexual identity formation: A theoretical model. *Journal of Homosexuality, 4*, 219–235. Retrieved from www.tandf.co.uk/journals/wjhm

Cass, V. C. (1996). Sexual orientation identity formation: A Western phenomenon. In R. P. Cabaj & T. S. Stein (Eds.), *Textbook of homosexuality and mental health* (pp. 227–251). Washington, DC: American Psychiatric Press.

Chapman, D. D., Shivji, M. S., Louis, E., Sommer, J., Fletcher, H., Prodöhl, P. A. (2007). Virgin birth in a hammerhead shark. *Biology Letters, 3*, 425–427. doi:10.1098/rsbl.2007.0189

Chasin, C. J. D. (2011). Theoretical issues in the study of asexuality. *Archives of Sexual Behavior, 40*, 713–723. doi:10.1007/s10508-011-9757-x

Chevigny, K., Davenport, B., Pinder, J. (Producers), & Tucker, A. (Director). (2011). *(A)sexual* [Documentary]. United States: Arts Engine.

Childs, D. (2009, January 16). Asexuals push for greater recognition. *ABC News*. Retrieved from http://abcnews.go.com/Health/MindMoodNews/asexuals-push-greater-recognition/story?id=6656358

Chivers, M. L. (2010). A brief review and discussion of sex differences in the specificity of sexual arousal. *Sexual and Relationship Therapy, 25*, 415–428. doi:10.1080/14681994.2010.518727

Chivers, M. L., Rieger, G., Latty, E., & Bailey, J. M. (2004). A sex difference in the specificity of sexual arousal. *Psychological Science, 11*, 736–744. doi:10.1111/j.0956-7976.2004.00750.x

Chivers, M. L., Seto, M. C., & Blanchard, R. (2007). Gender and sexual orientation differences in sexual response to sexual activities versus gender in sexual films. *Journal of Personality and Social Psychology, 93*, 1108–1121. doi:10.1037/0022-3514.93.6.1108

Christianson, G. E. (1984). *In the presence of the creator: Isaac Newton and his times*. New York: Free Press.

Clark, K. (1956). *The nude: A study in ideal form*. New York: Pantheon Books.

CNN.com. (2004, October 14). Study: One in 100 adults asexual. Retrieved from www.cnn.com/2004/TECH/science/10/14/asexual.study/index.html?iref=allsearch

Code of Canon Law. (n.d.). Chapter III: The obligations and rights of clerics. *IntraText CT*. Retrieved from www.intratext.com/IXT/ENG0017/_PX.HTM

Coleman, E. (1982). Developmental stages of the coming out process. *Journal of Homosexuality, 7*, 31–43. doi:10.1300/J082v07n02_06

Comings, D. E., Muhleman, D., Johnson, J. P., & MacMurray, J. P. (2002). Parent-daughter transmission of the androgen receptor gene as an explanation of the effect of father absence on age of menarche. *Child Development, 73*, 1046–1051.

Copas, A. J., Wellings, K., Erens, B., Mercer, C. H., McManus, S., Fenton, K. A. C., Korovessis, C., Macdowall, W., Nanchahal, K., & Johnson, A. M. (2002). The accuracy of reported sensitive sexual behaviour in Britain: Exploring the extent of change 1990–2000. *Sexually Transmitted Infections, 78*, 26–30. doi:10.1136/sti.78.1.26\

Coren, S. (1993). *The left-hander syndrome*. New York: Vintage.

Cowen, R. (2005). *History of life* (4th ed.). Malden, MA: Blackwell.

Csicsery, G. P. (Producer, Director). (1993). *N is a number: A portrait of Paul Erdos* [Motion picture]. United States: Zala Films.

Curtis, K. S., & Contreras, R. J. (2006). Sex differences in electrophysiological and behavioral responses to NaCl taste. *Behavioral Neuroscience, 120,* 917–924. doi:10.1037/0735-7044.120.4.917

Daly, M., & Wilson, M. (1988). *Homicide.* New York: Aldine de Grugter.

Daly, M., Wilson, M., & Weghorst, S. J. (1982). Male sexual jealousy. *Ethology and Sociobiology, 3*(1), 11–27. doi:10.1016/0162-3095(82)90027-9

Darwent, C. (2008). The naked and the nude, Middlesbrough Institute of Modern Art [Review of art exhibition *The Naked and the Nude* at the Middlesbrough Institute of Modern Art]. www.independent.co.uk/arts-entertainment/art/reviews/the-naked-and-the-nude-middlesbrough-institute-of-modern-art-middlesbrough-913650.html

D'Augelli, A. R. (1991). Gay men and college: Identity processes and adaptations. *Journal of College School Development, 32,* 140–146. Retrieved from www.jcsdonline.org

Davey, S. G., Frankel, S., & Yarnell, J. (1997). Sex and death: Are they related? Findings from the Caerphilly Cohort Study. *BMJ, 315,* 1641–1644. Retrieved from www.jstor.org/stable/25176559

Davies, S. (2004). *Emily Bronte: Heretic.* London: Women's Press.

Dawkins, R. (1976). *The selfish gene.* New York: Oxford University Press.

Diamond, L. (2006). What we got wrong about sexual identity development: Unexpected findings from a longitudinal study of young women. In A. M. Omoto & H. S. Kurtzman (Eds.), *Sexual orientation and mental health: Examining identity and development in lesbian, gay, and bisexual people. Contemporary perspectives on lesbian, gay, and bisexual psychology* (pp. 73–94). Washington, DC: American Psychological Association.

Diamond, L. M. (2003a). New paradigms for research on heterosexual and sexual-minority development. *Journal of Clinical Child and Adolescent Psychology, 32,* 490–498. doi:10.1207/S15374424JCCP3204_1

Diamond, L. M. (2003b). What does sexual orientation orient? A biobehavioral model distinguishing romantic love and sexual desire. *Psychological Review, 110,* 173–192. doi:10.1037//0033-295X.110.1.173

Dimitropoulou, P., Lophatananon, A., Easton, D., Pocock, R., Dearnaley, D. P., Guy, M., Edwards, S., O'Brien, L., Hall, A., Wilkinson, R., Eeles, R., Muir, K. R. (2009). Sexual activity and prostate cancer risk in men diagnosed at a younger age. *BJU International, 103,* 178–185. doi:10.1111/j.1464-410X.2008.08030.x

Doyle, A. C. (2003). *The complete Sherlock Holmes.* Vol. 2. New York: Barnes and Noble Classics.

Drew, J. (2003). The myth of female sexual dysfunction and its medicalization. *Sexualities, Evolution & Gender, 5,* 89–96. doi:10.1080/14616660310001632563

Droser, M. L., & Gehling, J. G. (2008). Synchronous aggregate growth in an abundant new ediacaran tubular organism. *Science, 319,* 1660–1662. doi:10.1126/science.1152595

Dyer, G. (1985). *War: Past, present, and future.* New York: Crown.

Eastman, M. (1936). *Enjoyment of laughter.* New York: Halcyon House.

ED Pills. (2010, March 30). *Buy discount Cialis and enjoy a romantic weekend.* Retrieved March 24, 2011, from www.edpills.org/Cialis/buy-discount-cialis-and-enjoy-a-romantic-weekend.html

Eilperin, J. (2007, May 23). Female sharks can reproduce alone, researchers find. *Washington Post.* Retrieved on April 27, 2008, from www.washingtonpost.com/wp-dyn/content/article/2007/05/22/AR2007052201405.html

Ekins, R., & King, D. (2004). Rethinking "Who put the 'Trans' in Transgender?" Symposium contribution at the Eighth International Gender Dysphoria Conference, Manchester, England.

Ellis, L., & Ames, M. A. (1987). Neurohormonal functioning and sexual orientation: A theory of homosexuality-heterosexuality. *Psychological Bulletin, 101*, 233–258.

Eta Carinae. (2005, July 25). Masturbating A's: What do you think about when masturbating? [Online forum post]. Retrieved from www.asexuality.org/en/index.php?/topic/9980-masturbating-as-what-do-you-think-about-when-masturbating

Fahs, B. (2010). Radical refusals: On the anarchist politics of women choosing asexuality. *Sexualities, 13*, 445–461. doi:10.1177/1363460710370650

Fausto-Sterling, A. (1993, March/April). The five sexes: Why male and female are not enough. *The Sciences*, 20–24.

Fausto-Sterling, A. (2000). The five sexes, revisited—The emerging recognition that people come in bewildering sexual varieties is testing medical values and social norms. *Sciences (New York), 40*(4), 18–23.

Federal Bureau of Investigation. (2002). Uniform crime reports. Retrieved January 29, 2007, from www.fbi.gov/about-us/cjis/ucr/ucr

Feinberg, L. (1992). *Transgender liberation: A movement whose time has come.* New York: World View Forum.

Ferguson, M. A., & Ford, T. E. (2008). Disparagement humor: A theoretical and empirical review of psychoanalytic, superiority, and social identity theories. *Humor, 21*, 283–312. doi:10.1515/HUMOR.2008.014

Fisher, H. (2004). *Why we love: The nature and chemistry of romantic love.* New York: Henry Holt.

Fisher, S. (1973). *The female orgasm: Psychology, physiology, fantasy.* New York: Basic Books.

Fishman, J. R. (2004). Manufacturing desire: The commodification of female sexual dysfunction. *Social Studies of Science, 34*, 187–218. doi:10.1177/0306312704043028

Fishman, J. R. (2007). Making Viagra: From impotence to erectile function. In A. Tone & E. S. Watkins (Eds.), *Medicating modern America: Prescription drugs in history* (pp. 229–252). New York: New York University Press.

Floyd, F. J., & Bakeman, R. (2006). Coming-out across the life course: Implications and historical context. *Archives of Sexual Behavior, 35*(3), 287–296. doi:10.1007/s10508-006-9022-x

Floyd, F. J., & Stein, T. S. (2002). Sexual orientation identity formation among gay, lesbian, and bisexual youths: Multiple patterns of milestone experiences. *Journal of Research on Adolescence, 12*, 167–191. doi:10.1111/1532-7795.00030

Fox, R. C. (1995). Bisexual identities. In A. R. D'Augelli & C. J. Patterson (Eds.), *Lesbian, gay, and bisexual identities over the lifespan: Psychological perspectives* (pp. 48–86). New York: Oxford University Press.

Freud, S. (1960). *Jokes and their relation to the unconscious.* J. Strachey, trans. New York: W. W. Norton. (Original work published 1905).

Freund, K., & Blanchard, R. (1993). Erotic target location errors in male gender dysphorics, pedophiles, and fetishists. *British Journal of Psychiatry, 162*, 558–563. doi:10.1192/bjp.162.4.558

Fulbright, Y. (2009, January 12). FOXSexpert: Asexuality—Is it even real? *Fox News.com.* Retrieved from www.foxnews.com/story/0,2933,479524,00.html

Gerressu, M., Mercer, C. H., Graham, C. A., Wellings, K., & Johnson, A. M. (2008). Prevalence of masturbation and associated factors in a British national probability survey. *Archives of Sexual Behavior, 37*, 266–278. doi:10.1007/s10508-006-9123-6

Gervais, M., & Wilson, D. S. (2005). The evolution and functions of laughter and humor: A synthetic approach. *Quarterly Review of Biology, 80*, 395–430. doi:10.1086/498281

Ghose, T. (2011, July 18). Asexual ants have sex. *The Scientist.* Retrieved from http://the-scientist.com/2011/07/18/asexual-ants-have-sex

Gilbert, G., Levy-Hinte, J., Rattray, C., Horowitz, J., Lundberg, D. T., Hellmann, P. (Producers), & Cholodenko, L. (Director). (2010). *The kids are alright* [Motion picture]. United States: Focus Features.

Grimbos, T., Dawood, K., Burriss, R. P., Zucker, K. J., & Puts, D. A. (2010). Sexual orientation and the second to fourth finger length ratio: A meta-analysis in men and women. *Behavioral Neuroscience, 124*, 278–287. doi:10.1037/a0018764

Grunt, J. A., & Young, W. C. (1952). Psychological modification of fatigue following orgasm (ejaculation) in the male guinea pig. *Journal of Comparative & Physiological Psychology, 45*, 508–510. doi:10.1037/h0063596

Hamer, D. H., Hu, S., Magnuson, V. L., Hu, N., & Pattatucci, A. M. L. (1993). A linkage between DNA markers on the X-chromosome and male sexual orientation. *Science, 261*(5119), 321–327. doi:10.1126/science.8332896

Hare, L., Bernard, P., Sánchez, F. J., Baird, P. N., Vilain, E., Kennedy, T., & Harley, V. R. (2009). Androgen receptor repeat length polymorphism associated with male-to-female transsexualism. *Biological Psychiatry, 65*, 93–96.

Hazan, C., & Shaver, P. (1987). Romantic love conceptualized as an attachment process. *Journal of Personality and Social Psychology, 52*, 511–524. Retrieved from www.apa.org/pubs/journals/psp/index.aspx

Hecox, M. J. (n.d.). Interview: Ten percent society celebrates 25 years [Web log post]. Retrieved from http://trueendeavorsblog.com/2008/11/11/interview-ten-percent-society-celebrates-25-years

Heiman, J. R. (1977). A psychophysiological exploration of sexual arousal patterns in females and males. *Psychophysiology, 14*, 266–274. doi:10.1111/j.1469-8986.1977.tb01173.x

Henningsson, S., Westberg, L., Nilsson, S., Lundström, B., Ekselius, L., Bodlund, O., Lindstrom, E., Hellstrand, M., Rosmond, R., & Eriksson, E. (2005). Sex steroid-related genes and male-to-female transsexualism. *Psychoneuroendocrinology, 30*, 657–664.

Hepper, P. G., Shabidullah, S., & White, R. (1991). Handedness in human fetus. *Neuropsychologia, 36*, 531–534.

Herek, G. M. (2000). The psychology of sexual prejudice. *Current Directions in Psychological Science, 9*, 19–22. doi:10.1111/1467-8721.00051

Herek, G. M. (2002). Gender gaps in public opinion about lesbians and gay men. *Public Opinion Quarterly, 66*, 40–66. doi:10.1086/338409

Heriot, A. (1956). *The castrati in opera.* London: Da Capo Press.

Hill, S. E., & Durante, K. M. (2011). Courtship, competition, and the pursuit of attractiveness: Mating goals facilitate health-related risk taking and strategic risk suppression in women. *Personality and Social Psychology Bulletin, 37*, 383–394. doi:10.1177/0146167210395603

Hirschfeld, M. (1948). *Sexual anomalies.* New York: Emerson Books.

Hobbes, T. (1840). Human nature. In W. Molesworth (Ed.), *The English works of Thomas Hobbes of Malmesbury* (Vol. 4). London: Bohn.

Hodson, G., Rush, J., & MacInnis, C. C. (2010). A joke is just a joke (except when it isn't): Cavalier humor beliefs facilitate the expression of group dominance motives. *Journal of Personality and Social Psychology, 99*(4), 660–682. doi:10.1037/a0019627

Hoffman, P. (1998). *The man who loved only numbers: The story of Paul Erdos and the search for mathematical truth.* New York: Hyperion.

Hyde, J. S., DeLamater, J. D., & Byers, E. S. (2009). *Understanding human sexuality* (4th Canadian ed.). Toronto: McGraw-Hill.

IBNLive.com. (2011, April 2). Archie comics plans for 1st gay character. Retrieved from http://ibnlive.in.com/news/archie-comics-plans-series-for-1st-gay-character/148026-40-100.html

Iemmola, F., & Camperio-Ciani, A. (2009). New evidence of genetic factors influencing sexual orientation in men: Female fecundity increase in the maternal line. *Archives of Sexual Behavior, 38*, 393–399. doi:10.1007/s10508-008-9381-6

Johnson, A. M., Mercer, C. H., Erens, B., Copas, A. J., McManus, S., Wellings, K., Fenton, K. A., Korovessis, C., Macdowall, W., Nanchahal, K., Purdon, S., & Field, H. (2001). Sexual behavior in Britain: Partnerships, practices, and HIV risk behaviors. *Lancet, 358*, 1835–1842. doi:10.1016/S0140-6736(01)06883-0

Johnson, A. M., Wadsworth, J., Wellings, K., & Field, J. (1994). *Sexual attitudes and lifestyles.* Oxford, UK: Blackwell Scientific Publications.

Joloza, T., Evans, J., & O'Brien, R. (2010, September). Measuring sexual identity: An evaluation report. UK Office of National Statistics.

Kelly, G. A. (1955). *The psychology of personal constructs.* New York: Norton.

Kinsey, A. C., Pomeroy, W. B., & Martin, C. E. (1948). *Sexual behavior in the human male.* Philadelphia: W. B. Saunders.

Kinsey, A. C., Pomeroy, W. B., Martin, C. E., & Gebhard, P. H. (1953). *Sexual behavior in the human female.* Philadelphia: W. B. Saunders.

Kopsida, E., Stergiakouli, E., Lynn, P. M., Wilkinson, L. S., & Davies, W. (2009). The role of Y chromosome in brain function. *Open Neuroendocrinology Journal, 2*, 20–30. Retrieved from www.benthamscience.com/open/toneuroej/index.htm

Kotula, D. (2002). A conversation with Dr. Milton Diamond. In *The phallus palace: The female to male transsexual* (pp. 35–56). Los Angeles: Alyson Publications.

Lalumière, M. L., Blanchard, R., & Zucker, K. J. (2000). Sexual orientation and handedness in men and women: A meta-analysis. *Psychological Bulletin, 126*, 575–592.

Lamberts, S. W. J., van den Beld, A. W., & van der Lely, A. J. (1997). The endocrinology of aging. *Science, 278*(5337), 419–424. doi:10.1126/science.278.5337.419

Langlois, J. H., Roggman, L. A., Casey, R. J., & Ritter, J. M. (1987). Infant preferences for attractive faces: Rudiments of a stereotype? *Developmental Psychology, 23*, 363–369. doi:10.1037//0012-1649.23.3.363

Laumann, E. O., Gagnon, J. H., Michael, R. T., & Michaels, S. (1994). *The social organization of sexuality.* Chicago: University of Chicago Press.

Laumann, E. O., Paik, A., & Rosen, R. C. (1999). Sexual dysfunction in the United States: Prevalence and predictors. *Journal of the American Medical Association, 281*, 537–544. doi:10.1001/jama.281.6.537

Lawler, S. (2008). *Identity: Sociological perspectives.* Cambridge, UK: Polity Press.

Lawrence, A. A. (2011). Autogynephilia: An underappreciated paraphilia. *Advances in Psychosomatic Medicine, 31*, 135–148. doi:10.1159/000328921

Leary, M. R., & Tangney, J. P. (Eds.). (2003). *Handbook of self and identity.* New York: Guilford Press.

Lerner, M. J. (1980). *The belief in a just world: A fundamental delusion.* New York: Plenum.

LeVay, S. (1991). A difference in hypothalamic structure between heterosexual and homosexual men. *Science, 253,* 1034–1037. doi:10.1126/science.1887219

LeVay, S. (2010). *Gay, straight, and the reason why: The science of sexual orientation.* New York: Oxford University Press.

Long, J. A., Trinajstic, K., & Johanson, Z. (2009). Devonian arthrodire embryos and the origin of internal fertilization in vertebrates. *Nature, 457,* 1124–1127. doi:10.1038/nature07732

Longley, R. (n.d.). On an "average" American day: BLS reports latest American time use survey. Retrieved from http://usgovinfo.about.com/od/censusandstatistics/a/averageday.htm

Louderback, L. A., & Whitley, B. E. (1997). Perceived erotic value of homosexuality and sex-role attitudes as mediators of sex differences in heterosexual college students' attitudes toward lesbians and gay men. *Journal of Sex Research, 34,* 175–182. Retrieved from www.tandfonline.com/toc/hjsr20/current

Lumsden, C., & Wilson, E. (1981). *Genes, mind and culture: The coevolutionary process.* Cambridge, MA: Harvard University Press.

MacInnis, C. C., & Hodson, G. (in press). Dehumanization and prejudice toward homosexuals, bisexuals, and asexuals. Poster presented at the Annual Meeting of the Canadian Psychological Association, Toronto, Canada.

Manning, J. T. (2002). *Digit ratio: A pointer to fertility, behavior, and health.* New Brunswick, NJ: Rutgers University Press.

Marmor, J. (1980). The multiple roots of homosexual behavior. In J. Marmor (Ed.), *Homosexual behavior: A modern reappraisal* (pp. 3–22). New York: Basic Books.

Martin, R. A. (2007). *The psychology of humor: An integrative approach.* Burlington, MA: Elsevier Academic Press.

Masters, W. H., & Johnson, V. (1966). *Human sexual response.* Boston: Little Brown.

Mathews, D. J. H., Bok, H., & Rabins, P. V. (2009). *Personal identity and fractured selves: Perspectives from philosophy, ethics, and neuroscience.* Baltimore: John Hopkins University Press.

Mazur, A. (1986). U.S. trends in feminine beauty and over-adaptation. *Journal of Sex Research, 22,* 281–303. doi:10.1080/00224498609551309

McGraw, A. P., & Warren, C. (2010). Benign violations: Making immoral behavior funny. *Psychological Science, 21,* 1141–1149. doi:10.1177/0956797610376073

Medland, S. E., Duffy, D., Spurdle, A., Wright, M., Geffen, G., Montgomery, G., & Martin, N. (2005). Opposite effects of androgen receptor CAG repeat length on increased risk of left-handedness in males and females. *Behavior Genetics, 35,* 735–744.

Meyer, I. H. (2003). Prejudice, social stress, and mental health in lesbian, gay, and bisexual populations: Conceptual and research evidence. *Psychological Bulletin, 129,* 674–697. doi:10.1037/0033-2909.129.5.674

Meyer-Bahlburg, H. F. (1977). Sex hormones and male homosexuality in comparative perspective. *Archives of Sexual Behavior, 6,* 297–325.

Money, J. (1988). *Gay, straight, and in-between.* New York: Oxford University Press.

Money, J. (1994). *Reinterpreting the unspeakable: Human sexuality 2000: The complete interviewer and clinical biographer, exigency theory, and sexology for the third millennium.* New York: Continuum.

Money, J., Hampson, J. G., & Hampson, J. L. (1957). Imprinting and the establishment of gender role. *Archives of Neurology and Psychiatry, 77*, 333–336. Retrieved from http://archneurpsyc.ama-assn.org

Morokoff, P. J. (1986). Volunteer bias in the psychophysiological study of female sexuality. *Journal of Sex Research, 22*, 35–51. Retrieved from www.jstor.org/stable/3812110

Morrell, J. P. (2006). *Between the lines: Master the subtle elements of fiction writing.* Cincinnati, OH: Writer's Digest Books.

Moser, C., & Kleinplatz, P. J. (2005). DSM-IV-TR and the paraphilias: An argument for removal. *Journal of Psychology and Human Sexuality, 17*, 91–109. Retrieved from www.tandfonline.com/toc/wzph20/current

Mosher, W. D., Chandra, A., & Jones, J. (2005). *Sexual behavior and selected health measures: Men and women 15-44 years of age, United States, 2002* [Advance Data From Vital and Health Statistics No. 362]. Hyattsville, MD: National Center for Health Statistics.

Motley, M. T., & Camden, C. T. (1985). Nonlinguistic influences on lexical selection: Evidence from double entendres. *Communication Monographs, 52*(2), 124–135. Retrieved from www.tandf.co.uk/journals/rcmm

National Centre for Social Research, Johnson, A., Fenton, K. A., Copas, A., Mercer, C., McCadden, A., Carder, C., Ridgway, G., Wellings, K., Macdowall, W., & Nanchahal, K. (2005). *National Survey of Sexual Attitudes and Lifestyles II, 2000–2001* [data file]. Colchester, Essex: UK Data Archive.

NNDB.com. Paul Erdos profile page. (2011). Retrieved from www.nndb.com/people/401/000032305

Nurius, P. S. (1983). Mental health implications of sexual orientation. *Journal of Sex Research, 19*, 119–136. Retrieved from www.jstor.org/stable/3812493

Parish, W. L., Das, A., & Laumann, E. O. (2006). Sexual harassment of women in urban China. *Archives of Sexual Behavior, 35*, 411–425. doi:10.1007/s10508-006-9079-6

Parish, W. L., Laumann, E. O., Cohen, M. S., Pan, S. M., Zheng, H. Y., Hoffman, I., Wang, T. F., & Ng, K. H. (2003). Population-based study of chlamydial infection in China—A hidden epidemic. *Journal of the American Medical Association, 289*, 1265–1273. doi:10.1001/jama.289.10.1265

Parish, W. L., Luo, Y., Laumann, E. O., Kew, M., & Yu, Z. Y. (2007). Unwanted sexual activity among married women in urban China. *Journal of Sex Research, 44*, 158–171. Retrieved from www.tandfonline.com/toc/hjsr20/current

Perkins, A., Fitzgerald, J. A., & Price, E. O. (1992). Luteinizing hormone and testosterone response of sexually active and inactive rams. *Journal of Animal Science, 70*, 2086–2093. Retrieved from http://jas.fass.org

Poikolainen, K., Kanerva, R., Marttunen, M., & Lönnqvist, J. (2001). Defence styles and other risk factors for eating disorders among female adolescents: A case-control study. *European Eating Disorders Review, 9*(5), 325–334. doi:10.1002/erv.407

Poston, D. L., Jr., & Baumle, A. K. (2010). Patterns of asexuality in the United States. *Demographic Research, 23*, 509–530. doi:10.4054/DemRes.2010.23.18

Prause, N., & Graham, C. A. (2007). Asexuality: Classification and categorization. *Archives of Sexual Behavior, 36*, 341–356. doi:10.1007/s10508-006-9142-3

Prerost, F. J. (1995). Sexual desire and the dissipation of anger through humor appreciation—gender and content issues. *Social Behavior and Personality, 23*, 45–52. Retrieved from www.sbp-journal.com

Provine, R. R. (2000). *Laughter: A scientific investigation.* New York: Viking.

Rabeling, C., Gonzales, O., Schultz, T. R., Bacci, M., Garcia, M. V. B., Verhaagh, M., Ishak, H. D., & Mueller, U. G. (2011). Cryptic sexual populations account for genetic diversity and ecological success in a widely distributed, asexual fungus-growing ant. *PNAS, 108,* 12366–12371. doi:10.1073/pnas.1105467108

Rellini, A., & Meston, C. (2007). Sexual function and satisfaction in adults based on the definition of child sexual abuse. *Journal of Sexual Medicine, 4,* 1312–1321.

Ridley, M. (1995). *The red queen: Sex and the evolution of human nature.* London: Penguin Books.

Rieger, G., Linsenmeier, J. A. W., Gygax, L., & Bailey, J. M. (2008). Sexual orientation and childhood gender nonconformity: Evidence from home videos. *Developmental Psychology, 44,* 46–58. doi:10.1037/0012-1649.44.1.46

Rind, B., Tromovitch, P., & Bauserman, R. (1998). A meta-analytic examination of assumed properties of child sexual abuse using college samples. *Psychological Bulletin, 124,* 22–53. doi:10.1037/0033-2909.124.1.22

Rohleder, H. (1907). *Vorlesungen über geschlechstrieb und gesamtes geschlechsleben des menschen* (Lectures on sexual drive and the complete sexual life of man). Vol. 2. Berlin: Fishers medizinsiche Buchhandlug/H. Kornfield.

Ronay, R., & von Hippel, W. (2010). The presence of an attractive woman elevates testosterone and physical risk taking in young men. *Social Psychological and Personality Science, 1,* 57–64. doi:10.1177/1948550609352807

Roselli, C. E., Larkin, K., Resko, J. A., Stellflug, J. N., & Stormshak, F. (2004). The volume of a sexually dimorphic nucleus in the ovine medial preoptic area/anterior hypothalamus varies with sexual partner preference. *Endocrinology, 145,* 478–483. doi:10.1210/en.2003-1098

Roselli, C. E., Larkin, K., Schrunk, J. M., & Stormshak, F. (2004). Sexual partner preference, hypothalamic morphology and aromatase in rams. *Physiology & Behavior, 83,* 233–245. doi:10.1016/j.physbeh.2004.08.017

Roselli, C. E., Stormshak, F., Stellflug, J. N., & Resko, J. A. (2002). Relationship of serum testosterone concentrations to mate preferences in rams. *Biology of Reproduction, 67*(1), 263–268. doi:10.1095/biolreprod67.1.263

Rosen, R., Brown, C., Heiman, J., Leiblum, S., Meston, C., Shabsigh, R., Ferguson, D., & D'Agostino, R. (2000). The Female Sexual Function Index (FSFI): A multidimensional self-report instrument for the assessment of female sexual function. *Journal of Sex & Marital Therapy, 26,* 191–208. doi:10.1080/009262300278597

Ross, L., Greene, D., & House, P. (1977). The false consensus effect—Egocentric bias in social-perception and attribution processes. *Journal of Experimental Social Psychology, 13,* 279–301. doi:10.1016/0022-1031(77)90049-X

Rothblum, E. D., & Brehony, K. A. (Eds.). (1993). *Boston marriages: Romantic asexual relationships among contemporary lesbians.* Amherst, MA: University of Massachusetts Press.

Roughgarden, J. (2004). *Evolution's rainbow: Diversity, gender, and sexuality in nature and people.* Berkeley: University of California Press.

Rubin, Z. (1973). *Liking and loving: An invitation to social psychology.* New York: Holt, Rinehart & Winston.

Ruscher, J. B. (2001). The culture of prejudice. In J. B. Ruscher (Ed.), *Prejudiced communication: A social psychological perspective* (pp. 173–201). New York: Guilford Press.

Rust, P. (1993). Coming out in the age of social constructionism: Sexual identity formation among lesbians and bisexual women. *Gender and Society, 7,* 50–77. doi:10.1177/089124393007001004

Saunders, D. M., Fisher, W. A., Hewitt, E. C., & Clayton, J. P. (1985). A method for empirically assessing volunteer selection effects: Recruitment procedures and responses to erotica. *Journal of Personality and Social Psychology, 49*, 1703–1712. Retrieved from www.apa.org/pubs/journals/psp/index.aspx

Scarr, S. (1987). Three cheers for behavior genetics: Winning the war and losing our identity: A presidential address to the Behavior Genetics Association. *Behavior Genetics, 17*, 219–228. doi:10.1007/BF01065502

Schank, R. C., & Abelson, R. P. (1977). *Scripts, plans, goals, and understanding.* Hillsdale, NJ: Erlbaum.

Schechter, B. (1998). *My brain is open: The mathematical journeys of Paul Erdos.* New York: Simon & Schuster.

Scherrer, K. S. (2008). Coming to an asexual identity: Negotiating identity, negotiating desire. *Sexualities, 11*, 621–641.

Sell, R. L., Wells, J. A., & Wypij, D. (1995). The prevalence of homosexual behavior and attraction in the United States, the United Kingdom and France—Results of national population-based samples. *Archives of Sexual Behavior, 24*, 235–248. doi:10.1007/BF01541598

Seto, M. C. (2008). *Understanding pedophilia and sexual offending against children: Theory, assessment, and intervention.* Washington, DC: American Psychological Association.

Seto, M. C., Cantor, J. M., & Blanchard, R. (2006). Child pornography offenses are a valid diagnostic indicator of pedophilia. *Journal of Abnormal Psychology, 115*, 610–615. doi:10.1037/0021-843X.115.3.610

Sigusch, V. (1998). The neosexual revolution. *Archives of Sexual Behavior, 27*, 339–351. doi:10.1023/A:1018715525493

Smith, A. M., Rissel, C. E., Richters, J., Grulich, A. E., & de Visser, R. O. (2003). Sex in Australia: Sexual identity, sexual attraction and sexual experience among a representative sample of adults. *Australian and New Zealand Journal of Public Health, 27*, 138–145.

Smuts, A. (2009, April 12). *Humor.* Retrieved April 12, 2011, from www.iep.utm.edu/humor

Spencer, H. (1860). The physiology of laughter. *Macmillan's Magazine, 1*, 395–402.

Sports Illustrated Media Kit for Advertisers: Swimsuit. (n.d.). *Sports Illustrated.* Retrieved April 16, 2011, from www.simediakit.com/property-single.xhtml?property_id=36

Stevens, R. (1983). *Erik Erikson: An introduction.* New York: St. Martin's.

Storms, M. D. (1980). Theories of sexual orientation. *Journal of Personality and Social Psychology, 38*, 783–792. doi:10.1037/0022-3514.38.5.783

Storms, M. D. (1981). A theory of erotic orientation development. *Psychological Review, 88*, 340–353. doi:10.1037/0033-295X.88.4.340

Symons, D. (1979). *The evolution of human sexuality.* New York: Oxford University Press.

Teddy Miller. (2005, July 25). Masturbating A's: What do you think about when masturbating? [Online forum post]. Retrieved from www.asexuality.org/en/index.php?/topic/9980-masturbating-as-what-do-you-think-about-when-masturbating

Terry, J. (1999). *An American obsession: Science, medicine, and homosexuality in modern society.* Chicago: University of Chicago Press.

Tiefer, L. (2002). Beyond the medical model of women's sexual problems: A campaign to resist the promotion of "female sexual dysfunction." *Sexual and Relationship Therapy, 17*, 127–135. doi:10.1080/14681990220121248

Trivers, R. L. (1972). Parental investment and sexual selection. In B. Campbell (Ed.), *Sexual selection and the descent of man* (pp. 136–179). Chicago: Aldine Atherton.

Troiden, R. R. (1989). The formation of homosexual identities. *Journal of Homosexuality, 17*, 43–73. Retrieved from www.tandf.co.uk/journals/wjhm

Udry, J. R., Billy, J. O. G., Morris, N. M., Groff, T. R., & Raj, M. H. (1985). Serum androgenic hormones motivate sexual behavior in adolescent boys. *Fertility and Sterility, 43*, 90–94. Retrieved from www.fertstert.org

Van Valen, L. (1973). A new evolutionary law. *Evolutionary Theory, 1*, 1–30. Retrieved from http://leighvanvalen.com/evolutionary-theory

Vasey, P. L., & VanderLaan, D. P. (2010). An adaptive cognitive dissociation between willingness to help kin and nonkin in Samoan Fa'afafine. *Psychological Science, 21*, 292–297.

Veale, J. F. (2008). Prevalence of transsexualism among New Zealand passport holders. *Australian and New Zealand Journal of Psychiatry, 42*(10), 887–889. doi:10.1080/00048670802345490

Ventegodt, S. (1998). Sex and quality of life in Denmark. *Archives of Sexual Behavior, 28*, 295–307. Retrieved from www.springer.com/psychology/personality+%26+social+psychology/journal/10508

Vicious Trollop. (2005, July 25). Masturbating A's: What do you think about when masturbating? [Online forum post]. Retrieved from www.asexuality.org/en/index.php?/topic/9980-masturbating-as-what-do-you-think-about-when-masturbating/page__p__237288#entry237288

Voeller, B. R. (1990). Some uses and abuses of the Kinsey scale. In D. P. McWhirter, S. Saunders, & J. Reinisch (Eds.), *Homosexuality-heterosexuality: Concepts of sexual orientation* (pp. 32–38). New York: Oxford University Press.

The Waitresses. (n.d.). I know what boys like. *Lyrics007*. www.lyrics007.com/Waitresses%20Lyrics/I%20Know%20What%20Boys%20Like%20Lyrics.html

Walsh, P. C. (2004). Ejaculation frequency and subsequent risk of prostate cancer. *Journal of Urology, 172*, 1552–1552. Retrieved from www.jurology.com

Westphal, S. P. (2004, October). Glad to be A. *New Scientist, 184*, 40–43.

White, M. (1999). *Isaac Newton: The last sorcerer.* Reading, MA: Helix Books.

Wild, M., & Argent, K. (1998). *Miss Lily's fabulous pink feather boa.* New York: Viking

Wilson, G., & Rahman, Q. (2005). *Born gay: The psychobiology of sex orientation.* London: Peter Owen Publishers.

Wilson, M., & Daly, M. (2004). Do pretty women inspire men to discount the future? *Proceedings of the Royal Society of London Series B—Biological Sciences, 271*, S177–S179. doi:10.1098/rsbl.2003.0134

Witelson, S. F., & Nowakowski, R. S. (1991). Left out axons make men right: A hypothesis for the origin of handedness and functional asymmetry. *Neuropsychologia, 29*, 327–333.

Wolf, N. (1991). *Beauty myth: How images of beauty are used against women.* New York: William Morrow.

World Health Organization. (n.d.). *Sexual and reproductive health: Gender and human rights.* Retrieved March 20, 2011, from www.who.int/reproductivehealth/topics/gender_rights/sexual_health/en

World Health Organization. (1992). *International statistical classifications of diseases and related health problems, 1989 revision.* Geneva: Author.

Yule, M. A. (2011). *Furthering our understanding of asexuality: An investigation into biological markers of asexuality, and the development of the asexuality identification scale* (Unpublished master's thesis). University of British Columbia, Vancouver.

Zillmann, D., & Bryant, J. (1980). Misattribution theory of tendentious humor. *Journal of Experimental Social Psychology, 16*(2), 146–160. doi:10.1016/0022-1031(80)90005-0

Zucker, K. J., & Bradley, S. J. (1995). *Gender identity disorder and psychosexual problems in children and adolescents.* New York: Guilford Press.

Index